DON'T HATE THE PLAYER LEARN THE GAME

How to Spot "Ineligible" Eligible Bachelors

By Lyn Lewis, PhD

Chicago, Illinois

Front cover illustration by Damon Stanford

First Edition, First Printing

Printed in the United States of America

ISBN #: 1-934155-83-7

ISBN #: 978-1934-155-837

Contents

Acknowledgments

The preparation of this book started long before the idea of the book was formulated. It started with my parents, Mr. and Mrs. Rufus and Onita Lewis, who created a learning center in our home that promoted the art and skill of critical thinking, the joy of reading, the desire to learn, and the motivation to become the best that you can be for each of their nine children. Words are inadequate to express my love for them and the many blessings they bestowed upon me, most of which were simply because they were who they were. Although my father passed away in 1986 years ago at the age of 68 and my mother lives at the age of 92, their influence on my intellectual development and other aspects of my life are immeasurable and invaluable. The only words that come close to thanking my parents can only be expressed in a spiritual context: To God Be The Glory! Let me hasten to add that the content of the book is not traceable back to my parents. The idea rests solely with me and those whom I allowed to influence me to write this book. These influential persons and their connection to this book will be explained later. However, whatever skills, intellect, and abilities that resonate in these written words go back to the talents God gave me, the foundation my parents laid for me, and their belief in me.

I was blessed to have eight siblings, four sisters and four brothers: Rose Marie, James Harold "Bubba", Bennie Jean, Ann Louise, Rufus, Jr., Lavern, Paul Stanley, and Frederick "Fred" Dwight. Thank you for your contributions, either indirectly or directly, generally or specifically to this book. I need to give a special shout-out to Fred, my youngest sibling. I called him and emailed him morning, noon, and night with all kinds of requests. He was my production, marketing, and promotional adviser. He would proofread, rearrange chapters and poems, lift me up, motivate me, and help me to stay focused. Fred, your support and encouragement were incalculable. I know you will stay with me for the next book and the books that will follow thereafter. Lavern, thank you for your support in your own inimitable way. Because of your assistance, I was able to give the book my full and undivided attention. You are a faithful trooper. I need to give a special thank you to my great niece, Lolita Sanford, who has been my greatest cheerleader. I can hear her saying, "Auntie Lyn, I can't wait to read your book. I'm going to get all my friends to read it because I know they will learn a lot."

A special appreciation is extended to my cousins, Watson Lewis and his wife, Linda Staley Lewis, for their support during the most crucial years of this project. Watson would often call and ask, "How's our book coming?" I would respond, "It's coming." Watson, your loyalty and faith in me are rarely seen by anyone, especially a cousin. Thanks also for the countless conversations we had on many topics, all of which served to keep me keeping on with the book. Watson, if you were older, I would move you from cousin to uncle like I did with your father, George Lewis. But for now, just remain the cousin you are and all will always be well between the two of us.

I have a friend, confidant, intellectual sparring partner, and avid reader, Attorney Ivy Thomas Riley, who has been so consistent, so steadfast, so committed, and so dedicated to this project. She has been pivotal to this project, from the title to its completion. She has been my proofreader, legal adviser, comforter, and motivator. She never acted like she was tired or weary, even though I know sometimes she had to be. We have had some of the most spirited discussions imaginable about the style, content, and syntax of this book. Ivy, I really don't know if this project would have reached its completion without you. Your dedicated, meticulous approach to details, love for learning, and determination to "hang in there" with me will remain a part of my memory. You truly qualify to be on my "persons who have meant the most to me list" in my lifetime. You go, girl!

My friend, Earlene Knox, whom I have known since my undergraduate college days, read, critiqued, and evaluated my poems and my thinking about the typologies of players. Thank you, my friend. Your melodramatic style in expressing your ideas on different parts of the book was unforgettable and I greatly appreciated our lively conversations. Earlene, you really know how to make it interesting and challenging at the same time.

Attorney Richard Harris and his wife Dr. Marjorie Harris have been a key source of my strength in the completion of this book. You gave me words of wisdom, and spent your time, energy, and effort in helping me through this project as well as other areas of concern with which I was faced. Although you are in your '80s, you both spoke of the relevancy of this book in today's changing times. After reading a part of the book, Marjorie, you were convinced that the content will help women of all ages, including those in their '80s like you who are mothers, grandmothers, and great-grandmothers.

I did not set out to write this book. The data in this book came to me and made me write it. Now the question is, just how did the data make me write this book? Thanks to my "Super Star" students at the University of Detroit Mercy, I was able to collect some of the data for this book without knowing it at the time. Once a month, I held "Life Talk with Lyn Lewis." This allowed students to ask anonymous questions about anything in the field of sociology. Thus, anything that deals with the behavior of people was within the asking zone. Most of their questions were about men, women, and relationships. I began to compile the data for some future use, the specifics of which were beyond me at the time. The more we talked, the more I noticed that students' questions laid out a pattern that focused on noncommitted relationships. I examined the data and realized that there were patterns of behavior that fitted distinctive noncommitted categories. I then began to poetically describe some of the behavior that was reported in the questions and responses. The students lamented, "Dr. Lewis, you need to write a book on these men." These were the sparks of discourse that lit the formation of this book. Thank you, students for your inquisitiveness, your honesty, and your desire to have a much-needed discussion about a social phenomenon that affects almost all males and females. Your input is greatly appreciated.

A few years ago I took on the position of Adjunct Professor at Wayne County Community College District (WCCCD) and continued the monthly Life Talk in my classes. These "Super Star" students were also preoccupied with questions and discussions about men, women, and relationships. Their data are a part of this book as well. To all of my WCCCD students, thank you for your contributions to this book and your thoughts about the poems and the chapter titles. Your input helped to fully develop each of the categories of players.

In addition to the data collected from my students' Life Talk questions and responses, I kept records of my clients' complaints, problems, and issues during my years in private practice as a therapist. I also recorded the discourses that would occur during Friends First, an organization that was formed by three of my friends and colleagues and me. Data collected during male-female relationship workshops and seminars were retained as well. I would recall the most salient points from these sessions and store them for some future use. Thanks to all these clients and participants, this book started to take shape. To all the other men and women, from different walks of life who agreed to be interviewed and reveal their stories, thank you. Your time and cooperation are greatly appreciated.

The data collected for the Down Low Player chapter took on a slightly different approach because of the secrecy factor. I owe a big thank you to the males who first agreed to be interviewed and the other males they referred to me. Those males referred even more males to me. This data collection method is known as snowballing.

To the focus group participants, I thank you for all the time, energy, and serious discussions you contributed to this book. You critiqued each part of it with a high level of intellectual sophistication and a deep commitment to giving your best truth. That's all any author can ask of a focus group. You did me proud!

Keil Troisi and your company Scriptproof deserve a special thanks for your proofreading of the first and second drafts of this book. Thank you for your patience and understanding.

When I started this project, my affiliations with the social networks left a lot to be desired. I want to thank Dustin Barlow for teaching me about different social networks and connecting me to them. I hope your career continues to flourish and move upward and onward.

Last, to Dr. Jawanza Kunjufu who without hesitation, agreed to publish my book by his publishing company, African American Images, Inc. Your belief in me and this project will forever hold a place of high esteem in my life. You wasted no time in moving on everything that is needed during the final preparatory stages for publication. I will forever be grateful to you for all of your support in this endeavor. I want to especially thank Damon Stanford, the architect of artistic designs, for designing the beautiful illustration on the cover of my book. Even the designs that you developed that were not chosen in the final analysis were quite impressive to me. Keep up the great work! To the editing staff of African American Images, Inc., your quality editing of this book far exceeded my expectations. Your cooperation and critical perspectives were welcomed assets in getting to the finished product. You and your boss, Dr. Kunjufu, were treats with whom to work. Let's do this again with my next book!

If I overlooked anyone who made a contribution to this book, thank you for your support and charge my oversight to my head and not my heart.

Dedication

I dedicate this book to all players, "wanna be" players, and the women who get caught up in the players' game. I especially thank those players and the women they played who contributed to the completion of this book. Your usage of plain and simple English to explain players' behavior and the behavior of their victims make for a meaningful, insightful, and enjoyable reading. As you read it, ask yourself: Is this how I want to treat myself in relationships? Is this how I want others to treat me in relationships? Do I want to experience the social, emotional, physical, and moral consequences of my behavior? And last, if I continue with this lifestyle, what will my life experience feel like and look like as I grow older? Will I still want to be a player? Will I be the woman who continues to let men play me? The verdict is yours!

Introduction

Women, did you know that there are more than 45 million single men in the United States over the age of 21 who fall in the category of never married, widowed, or divorced? Did you know that some of these males are ineligible for a committed relationship? Did you know that some of them are ineligible for marriage? Labels that are not recorded in the US Census Bureau's definition of single but are a part of these men's marital status classification system are: ineligible, never will get married, never will want to get married, never will need to get married, "why buy the cow when you're getting the milk free" fear of loving in an intimate, sexual relationship, "variety is the spice of life", and non-heterosexual sexual orientations. These men will avoid a committed relationship probably more than they will avoid the plague. Their behavior suggests that they invented a philosophy in male-female relationships, either knowingly or unknowingly called "Much Right". This Much Right philosophy is based on men's belief that they have as much right as anyone else to hold whatever marital status they choose to hold whenever they choose to hold it. Utilizing interviews from single men who also defined themselves as players, this book explains why "single" does not automatically mean eligible. The point that will be made crystal clear is: ***Eligibility is a state of mind.***

When I shared with men and women that I was writing a book, the first question was, "What is the title?" I said, "Don't Hate the Player". Before I had the chance to say "Learn the Game", they would say, "Hate the Game", thinking that they were completing my title. In actuality, they were repeating the frequently used phrase, Don't hate the player, hate the game. Some tried to correct me by saying, it's not "Learn the Game", it's "Hate the Game". In this book, it is Learn the Game. What lessons have people learned from hating? It takes a lot of time, energy, and effort to hate. Hate almost always has a destructive ending. Hate is an emotion that can define a situation as despicable and deprecating and overshadow something that could have manifested in positive social consequences. To learn, on the other hand, is to acquire knowledge and gain insight about human behavior and social relationships. It is a step in the right direction that can lead to the development of skills, talents, and abilities needed to figure out and understand why men and women act the way they act. Why do men and women have problems sustaining relationships over time? And, how can men and women enhance their social relationships with each other? It is also a mental movement toward the acquisition of discernment and wisdom, two qualities that are critical to a sound, objective, and logical approach to the understanding of intimate, sexual relationships between men and women. Therefore, to hate the game is counterproductive and can very easily end in a devastating human train wreck.

About 10 years ago, the once a month Life Talk discussions I held in my college classes were in full swing. As usual, male-female relationships dominated the discourse. Most of the anonymous questions to which I responded were written by women about men with whom they were in a relationship. The questions were mainly the type that started with, "What should a woman do when a man does...." I answered each question to the best of my knowledge base. At the end of one of the classes, three males came up to me and said, "Dr. Lewis, you need to stop telling these women all the things you are telling them because if you keep this up, we will not be able run any game on them." My response was, "The purpose of Life Talk is to learn how to develop and sustain relationships that are meaningful and beneficial to both persons involved. The goal is to understand the social behavior of men and women in relationships so that the same relationship mistakes will not continue to be made. This can only happen through learning. You may want to rethink your game playing behavior and ask yourself, 'Why do I feel the need to play games in relationships?'" This book is about learning because to learn the game is to grow. To learn the game is to know more about your strengths and shortcomings and how to work to make your shortcomings your strengths. To learn the game is to put yourself in a position to develop all aspects of self-development. This is why this book will focus on learning the game, and ultimately understanding the game and how it is played before it is played on you.

The players illustrated in this book are ineligible bachelors who have no desire to engage in serious, committed, unmarried relationships or marriage. A common denominator of each of these players, regardless of the motive for their player behavior is their intimate and sexual involvement with more than one mate. The Truth Tellers are so confident in their ability to play games on several women at the same time, that over time they tell the women enough truth about their player agenda for the women to make an informed decision as to whether or not they are interested in continuing the relationship. Even when women state that they are only interested in a committed relationship that has a strong probability of moving to marriage, they more often than not continue the relationship with the player. This type of continuation causes men to develop the attitude that was expressed by one player when he was asked, "How is your love life?" He responded, "Any way I want it to be." Or as another player put it, "I don't approach a woman if I don't think I can master her. If I think I can master her, I will approach her. If I don't think I can master her, I will leave her alone." This book lets women know that women and only women can save themselves from being victimized by the Truth Teller players. If women are truly interested in saving themselves from male predators in intimate, sexually relationships, they must learn how to "keep their dress down and their knees together," as one man put it. Another man stated that what women need to do is "stop letting men keep them looking up at the ceiling," meaning, refrain from relationships that only have sex as its motivation for men. Still another man said that women "need to stop giving away so much a__. They need to understand that there is power in the p____y." Still another man said, "Women need to go on strike and stop having sex with men as soon as they meet them. They are giving it away like it grows on trees." He went on to say that women need to form a union called the "ISVC Union-The International Sisterhood of Vaginal Control-Local 1000." His position, along with that of many other players is, if women don't get control over their sexual encounters with men before the men have demonstrated that they deserve it, players have no reason to change their player ways.

The betrayers, the other group of players discussed in this book, are very difficult for women to recognize. They hide and deny their intentions with deceit and cover-ups. They orchestrate a well conceived, premeditated, methodical, calculating, and strategic plan to convince women that they are who they say they are, when in fact they are not. They are deceptive and manipulative because they know if they were to tell the truth about who they are and what their motives are, the likelihood is that they would not succeed in their quest to get what they want from women.

By now, some of you may be asking: How did men develop these attitudes that manifest in behavior that promotes a two or more mates mentality and denounces a one mate mentality? Some of this behavior can be traceable back to the teaching in the homes during the formative years of males and females. To demonstrate this double standard of sexual behavior based on gender roles, in my marriage and family classes, I would state a scenario that involved a father, mother, a nine-year-old daughter and a seven-year-old son. The son comes home and tells his parents, "I have this many girlfriends" and he holds up five fingers. His father lets out a big chuckle and says, "Chip off the old block." The mother says with a big smile on her face, "Oh, look at my son. He's so popular. What are their names?" The next day, the nine-year-old daughter comes home and says to her parents, "Mom, Dad, I have this many boyfriends" and she holds up three fingers. The dad goes ballistic and says, "Put those fingers down right now and I don't ever want you to talk about boyfriends until I give you permission and that will not happen until you are 18. And when that time comes, you will only have one boyfriend, not three. Hoes (whores) have three boyfriends at a time." He then tells her to go to her room, he takes all her privileges away and he grounds her for one month. The mother says, "Your father is telling you right. You are much too young to talk about boyfriends and I agree with everything your father said." As I discussed this gender difference with a male friend of mine, who's a legendary NFL former all-star quarterback, he informed me that when he was eight years old, his grandmother would tell his sister, who was 17, that she had to be home by 11:00 p.m. Then the grandmother would say, "Because you know that the only thing that's open in Monroe, Louisiana after 11:00 p.m. is legs." He noticed that his brother was never told to keep his pants up. He went on to say, "Lyn, you know in Monroe where we grew up, there were only three places you could go—to school, to church, and to football games. So if you stayed out after the football game was over, there was no lie to tell because there was no place for teenagers to go after 11:00 p.m." These different standards and verbal exchanges lay the foundation for the double standard to continue for years and decades in the lives of men and women.

Another key feature in this book is the manner in which the data from players and some of the women they played were collected. First, data were collected from hundreds of men and some women over the course of 15 years from therapy sessions, a singles group, classroom discussions, focus groups, seminars, and workshops. Some of them were interviewed formally or informally. Second, usually the researcher collects data on a predetermined area of concern. This was not the case with these data. As I examined the data over a period of time, some of the data formed a pattern. That pattern was identified by the males who expressed desires to engage in several intimate, sexual relationships at the same time and the women who complained about them. Third, these data revealed why players engaged in relationship games, and their motives, behavior, and benefits. Fourth, it uses popular culture language to promote a more enjoyable read and a most enlightening learning experience, irrespective of age, race, geographical location, and educational background. Young, middle age, and seniors will take a liking to it. These data lay out for women the raw truth about what men who define themselves as players think about women who tolerate and sometimes embrace their player behavior.

The unique structure of this book has another feature. It focuses on poems, surveys, self-rating and self-scoring scales, and "for real" pseudonyms of the players. At the beginning of each chapter, I poetically express the content of the chapter and illustrate the characteristics of the players described in it. The surveys, rating and scoring scales were designed to give you, the reader, an opportunity to take a personal, secretive analysis of your behavior in intimate, sexual relationships. They promote self-evaluation and self-assessment as ways to determine if a more formalized, professional therapeutic approach is needed. Each chapter ends with at least two 20-question surveys. I designed one for the males to determine if they fit the type of player in the chapter and one for the females to determine if they are involved with that type player. When the men and women tally their scores, they can determine if they fit in the category or the extent to which they fit. This type of inclusion affords you, the readers, the opportunity to make a valuation about the way you love, who you love, why you love or don't love, and if you are in need of a therapeutic approach to become healthier, joyous, and more prosperous in your intimate, sexual relationship. The pseudonyms were chosen to protect the identity of those who so graciously contributed to this book. They were also selected with the hope that they will raise the creative visualization of you, the readers, on the nature and type of these players.

At this point, it is glaringly clear that this book is about men, but it is written for women—and men, too.

Part I

The Truth Tellers

A common phrase women use to describe men in relationships whom they thought were on the path of commitment and possibly marriage, when in fact they were not is, “I didn’t know he was like that.” This phrase usually translates to mean that they did not recognize the signs of non-commitment in his behavior or that he led them to believe that he was the committed type. As noted earlier, this book is divided into two major categories: The Truth Tellers and The Betrayers. The Truth Tellers are composed of five sub-groups: The Gravy Train Player, The Mama’s Boy Player, The Smorgasbord Player, The Gas and Go Player, and the As-Is Player. These sub-groups and the typologies in each in no way exhaust the total categories of players, nor do pseudonyms deplete the groupings of each type player. They do lay a foundation on which other studies can expand the study of players’ behavior in a society with an appreciable number of singles, male and female.

Truth Teller Players have four characteristics in common. They tell women who they really are. They show women who they really are. They are noncommittal in their motives. And, they are willing to engage in sex with women on the first, second, and third encounters, and beyond. Sometimes these players brag about their sexual prowess to their friends and talk about what a player they are because they had unprotected sex with some women before they knew her first or last name. They brag about having unprotected sex with women who didn’t know their first or last name. They brag about having unprotected sex with women they just met. Among men, they talk about how women should wait until the man shows signs that he’s interested in her as a person and not as a sex object before they have sex.

One man, who is a father and grandfather talked about how he tells his daughter and granddaughter that men who are really interested in women as a total woman and not just someone to have sex with will wait for the sex. He went on to say, “I make sure my daughter and granddaughter know that there are stages in relationships and having sex is not the first stage. First, you’re just getting to know each other so you talk on the phone, text, or talk to each other on Facebook. Then, the man will ask you to go out with him to dinner, a movie, a concert, or some other entertainment. This is the dating stage. I make sure I let them know that sex is off-limits in this stage. I also let them know that if he doesn’t ask you to go to one of those places or somewhere similar, he is not interested in a relationship that can lead to commitment or marriage. When a man takes a woman out for the first time and takes her directly to a hotel or to his house and lets it be known that sex, and sex only, is on his agenda, that means that he’s looking for a booty call, only. Courting is the next stage. I tell them that this is when a woman should decide if she plans on staying in the relationship. The next progressive stage is engagement, and the final stage is marriage.

If a man doesn't want you to meet his family and friends and he doesn't want to meet yours, and he doesn't take you out, he probably is not interested in you as a significant female in his life." This man is trying to educate his daughter and granddaughter so that they don't become victimized by players.

Since these men tell the women who they are, they could not continue their player behavior without women who are willing to engage in intimate, sexual relationships with them. Therefore, these men's continuation of their sexual way of life is predicated on women who are willing participants in their sexual lifestyle.

Chapter 1

The Gravy Train Player

You're my desperado woman
I'm your well kept man
You want me so badly
Your head stays buried in the sand

You treat me like I'm your heart
Your most important part
Mr. Oxygen Pump is my name
Your arteries, tissues and veins
Testify to my claim to fame

You act like I'm your lungs
The reason for every breath you breathe
You place me on such a high pedestal
The sun and moon look up at me

I'm your central nervous system
I control the thoughts in your brains
You march to the beat of my drums
That's why I boarded your gravy train

You take care of me in grand style
You begged me to move in
You lavished me with clothes and jewels
And a shiny royal blue Mercedes Benz

People ask me why I live with you
The answer is very simple
Non-commitment
Convenience
And available sex
I'm the crowned king of your temple

If you ever ask me to chip in
Or help you pay the rent
I'll quickly let you know
I'm not giving your stupid a_ _
One measly red cent

You'll pay any price for my company
You'll gladly neglect your kids

You'll fight lions in their den
And commit the seven deadly sins

This gravy train I boarded
Travels at the speed of my sound
It jumps over tracks when I say jump
It slows down when I say slow down

I'm the sole passenger
On my woman's gravy train
Every compartment bears my name
That's how I got her tamed

Try to come aboard her train
If you don't believe my hype
She'll point to her big sign that reads
My train is full
All others take a hike

All Aboard

"Gravy, gravy everywhere; the female trains these men board, let them live free and charge no fare." I made the above statement during a forum about women who allow men to move in with them and provide them with free boarding, food, and clothing, and literally take care of them. This comment was made after a male in attendance stated that he had been living with his girlfriend for seven years. As he continued to talk about how good she has been to him, he bragged, "She bought me this suit. I like for her to buy my clothes. She has good taste. Don't you, baby?" He looked at her and she smiled back at him. Then he stated, "What I really like about her is that she loves pleasing me in every way she can. I love for her to please me. Don't I, baby?" The woman did not verbally respond. She sat there, smiling, and looked at him in the most "I adore you" manner. She did not appear to be the least bit embarrassed by what her male partner said about her. Another male replied, "He got him a meal ticket." A woman spoke out, saying, "He hit the jackpot. Meeting her was like coming into a windfall." Then two males stated, "Now he's sitting pretty." "He has it even better than that. That man has got him a gravy train." A female participant inquired, "So what is a gravy train?" A male responded, "That's when a man hits 'pay dirt' with a woman." The female then asked, "What's pay dirt?" A male explained that "pay dirt" is a term used by men when something really beneficial, desirable, favorable, and advantageous has occurred in their lives. In this case, it's a woman who is willing to play the role of his caregiver and caretaker. Still another man stated, "It's even better than that. He found his Home

Depot." A woman then said, "When I think of Home Depot, I think of the store." The male followed that with, "Yeah, Home Depot is a store. It prides itself on having everything people need and want to get their house in order. This woman is this man's Home Depot because she tries to take care of all his wants and his needs. She tries to have everything for him, just like a Home Depot tries to have everything for its customers."

To further clarify the concept used in this idiom, the words "gravy" and "train" were discussed separately and then as a concept that suggests that a man is being cared for by a woman in her home. A gravy train, in this context, refers to a male who has moved in with a woman for the purpose of being "kept" by her. "Kept" refers to her taking care of him, providing him with food, clothing, shelter, love, affection, and niceties and amenities such as a car, clothes, jewelry, and miscellaneous elements per his request. The male defines this as a very lucrative and rewarding arrangement for him, since his primary responsibilities are to be present and satisfy the woman sexually. He sees himself as a benefactor of her generosity or her stupidity or a combination of both. One male at the forum pointed out that the gravy train slogan is so popular, it also bears the name of a brand of dog food.

Another male said, "Yeah, I have a friend who was really a benefactor of a woman's generosity. This man had horrible looking teeth. The same man went on to say that his friend decided to move from the East Coast to the Midwest to be with her. Now, his teeth are cleaner, whiter, and stronger because she spends her money to take him to the dentist." He had about three teeth missing, one in the front and two on the side. His teeth looked like they had never been cleaned. She was a professional woman who felt she needed a man on her arm to look a certain way, so to fix his mouth to her specifications she paid for his dental work. She told me that he had three implants. Implants are expensive, but she paid for all the work. Then she had his teeth cleaned. He didn't look like the same person. Every time I saw him after that, he was smiling, showing his pearly white teeth.

Still another male talked about how his male friend had a "body-type transformation" when he moved in with his woman. He stood about 6' 2'' and weighed about 150 pounds. He looked malnourished. She started feeding him good and she got him to go to the spa with her to work out. I saw him about eight months after he moved in with her and I didn't recognize him. I have known him practically all my life and I have never known him to have muscles. He has muscles now and he looks healthy. I told him how good he looked and I asked him what he weighed. He told me he weighed about 190 pounds, but it was all muscles. Like that dog food commercial says, the gravy train can build strong bones. So maybe she believes that if she keeps him healthy, he will continue to have good sex with her. For women, the sex is the main thing that drives them to do what they do for a man. If he is not good in bed, she doesn't care how good he treats her, he has to go—quick, fast, and in a hurry. Therefore, the major requirement to getting on the female gravy train is to sexually satisfy her. As long as he keeps his sexual skills up to her liking, he can ride her female gravy train and all she will say is "choo choo."

Who Let the Dogs Out?

There are many clichés that are used to associate men's sexual promiscuity with dogs. In a discussion about men's behavior in intimate sexual relationships, you are sure to hear such phrases as, "men are dogs," or "all men are dogs," or "all men have some dog in them," or "it's the dog in men that makes them do wrong." These statements are not only echoed by women, they are stated vociferously by some men. As a matter of fact, some men make these statements with their chest stuck out, as if they are bragging about their sexual prowess. When these statements are made, it must be understood that the reference of men to dogs is related to men who cheat sexually on their mates. That is, they have sex with two or more women without divulging this to one or more of the women. In a Life Talk conversation about men who enjoy having indiscriminate sex with women, one male stated his case in a syllogism. He said, "All men are dogs. I'm a man. Therefore, I'm a dog, too." Another man took issue with his statement and stated, "I don't deny that there is some dog in all men, I just don't think that all men are dogs. I think men act like dogs toward women when women accept dog-like behavior from them. Women who don't accept dog-like behavior from men don't get it. If she acts like a lady, we treat her like a lady. If she acts like a hoe [whore], we treat her like one. How she wants to be treated is on her."

Another male disagreed with the above explanation. He replied, "I'm a man and I know I'm a dog. I'm really more like a wolf than a dog. I don't see myself changing because I don't want to change. I'm having too much fun the way I am and I believe in that saying, 'Once you have been a wolf, it's hard to step down and act like a goat.'" Notice the wording of this phrase, especially the part that says "step down". It suggests that a man acting like a goat is acting like he's less than a man. I asked the group to tell me what they thought was the difference between a wolf and a goat. One male responded, "A wolf is treacherous. He will do anything to anybody, whereas a goat is not out to harm anyone."

Another participant claimed, "A wolf is a predator. Any animal is fair game that crosses his path. It doesn't matter whether they are smaller or bigger than him, he's out to get them." To bring more credibility to the conversation, I pointed out that wolves, unlike goats, are carnivorous. They will kill and eat other animals at will, though mainly for food. They are wild animals and they will stake out their territory. Invaders are not allowed. Goats, on the other hand, are easy to handle, loyal, easy to train, pleasant, and followers, not leaders. A male then claimed, "I wouldn't say that men are as bad as wolves, but women don't want us to act like no goat and we don't want to act like one neither."

The language of men as dogs does not only resonate in male-female relationships, it is heard in the aesthetics of music and in the sports world. In 1998, Anslem Douglas wrote and originally recorded the song "Who Let the Dogs Out," from a Trinidad and Tobago's Carnival. Two years later, it was produced with a group known as the Baha Men. The popularity of this song exceeded anyone's expectations. It is commonplace to hear fans at a sports event chanting the title of the song, then making barking sounds of whoof, whoof, whoof, whoof, whoof. It's interesting to note that the song has received worldwide attention in male-dominated sports arenas. In the United States, Major League Baseball teams and National Football League teams use it frequently as a lyrical tool to get the crowd involved in the game and cheer for their favorite team. College teams such as Mississippi State University joined the bandwagon and chanted the lyrics at their football games. The Seattle Mariners is one of the teams most noted for their usage of it. At the 2000 World Series between the New York Mets and the New York Yankees, the chants of "Who Let the Dogs Out" were so frequent, it appeared to be both teams' theme song. How is it that a song with these lyrics caught on like wildfire and has commonly been heard in the institution of sports that is primarily dominated by men?

First, the word "dog" is used by some men as a slang greeting. The most likely groups of men to use these phraseologies are blue-collar workers and entertainers, especially in the music industry, non-political radio disc jockeys (DJs), and men in the sports industry. Oftentimes, these greetings are used in endearing ways and may speak to a close relationship between the users. You may hear a man say to another man, "What's up, dog?" Or, "You know you're my dog." Or, "That's my dog," referring to a male friend. The men who use these phrases embrace them and see them as complimentary statements and acceptable greetings. It should be noted that all men do not use these phrases. Upper middle class, professional, and top executive men, especially those who are outside of the sports world, are the most unlikely groups to use them.

The question that still remains is: Who let the dogs out? Did men let the dog out within themselves, since they are men and are held accountable for their behavior? Did those women who tolerate dog-like behavior from men let the dogs out? Are men and women jointly responsible for letting the dogs out? At a social workers' conference, I conducted a workshop on male-female relationships. During the workshop, I stated that women are so significant in the lives of heterosexual men that they will literally change whatever behavior they exhibit that is viewed as intolerable by women if women refuse to have sex with them. A male social worker raised his hand and stood up and said, "I am so glad you are letting these women know that because that is the truth. I have told women that if men who commit crimes were told and shown that because of their criminal behavior, women would not have sex with them, their illegal behavior will be no more. If drug dealers were unable to have sex with women because they were drug dealers, they would stop selling drugs." These comments received clamorous disagreements and a few agreements from both men and women.

One male stated, "I don't know where you get that from. Anything I want to do, I will do it. I don't care if women like it or not." I pointed out that the boycott of men's behavior would need to include all women. Women are more likely to live to the age of 150 than they are likely to unite holistically for a common cause against men. The topic had workshop participants talking so much and holding so many sidebar conversations that for a few moments, it was difficult to determine who was saying what. I stated, at this point, that even if women adhered to a *sexual moratorium,* there probably would be some men who would refuse to change their behavior. Also, what is the likelihood that women could hold a sexual moratorium for any length of time? At this point, one female participant stated, "If women decided to hold a sexual moratorium, don't count me in. Listen, I'm going to get my share of sex while I'm here on earth because you can't take it with you." When asked, "Take what with you?" She responded, "The enjoyment of sex and all that it gives me." When the workshop ended, there was an informal discussion that was just as lively as the formalized one. If all women stopped having sex with men because of some objectionable aspect of men's behavior, will there be a change in their behavior? We will never know. What we do know is that women need this dog alert: *Beware of dogs. They may have you howling!*

Gravy Train Ticket—Who's Eligible?

All men do not qualify to purchase a gravy train ticket and board the gravy train. These men must be of a certain breed to fit these eligibility requirements. Some major aspects of these criteria will be examined now.

Billy the Boll Weevil

First, they must have a *boll weevil mentality.* Upon introducing the boll weevil mentality concept at a seminar, a male asked, "What the hell is a boll weevil?" The other male replied, "Where are you from?" The guy said, "I'm from New Jersey." "Well, that explains it. I'm from Mississippi and I used to chop cotton and pick cotton. Sometimes the cotton crop wouldn't be that good because boll weevils, which are little beetles, had gotten inside the cotton ball and eaten the cotton. You see, the boll weevil is an insect that is so dangerous that it can destroy a whole crop of cotton. These little creatures spend their time always looking for a home." This man is a real Southerner.

In the male-female relationship vernacular, especially in the Deep South where cotton was one of the major crops, the boll weevil has taken on an interesting connotation. If a man is looking for a woman who will let him move in with her for free—at least as far as free applies to money—many Southerners will say, "He ain't nothing but a boll weevil, looking for a home." This line of thought was so pervasive in the South that blues songs were recorded to illustrate the meaning of the boll weevil.

It is clear at this point that one of the criteria required for qualifying as a gravy train ticket holder is that you must be like the boll weevil. You must be *looking for a home* or not voice any opposition to finding one.

George the Gift Benefactor

The second criterion is that they must have a *gift benefactor mentality.* The female gravy train will supply recipients with little-ticket and big-ticket items. These items may be as small as a toothbrush, comb, or razor and as expensive as a car, boat, or house. In a conversation with a male regarding the gifts he received from his female gravy train, he stated, "What man doesn't like gifts?" In another situation, a male was in therapy. His chief complaint was his troubled relationship with one of his children. During the course of the therapy sessions, he talked about the woman with whom he was living. He met her at a concert's afterglow party. He claimed that getting involved in a live-in relationship was not on his mind. But after a few dates and some sexual encounters, "She made me an offer I couldn't refuse. She told me that if I moved in with her, she would take care of me."

He gave up his apartment and moved into her home that was located in an upscale neighborhood and he began to benefit from her generosity immediately. He noted, "First, she gave me the keys to a BMW and told me it was mine to keep. Then she took me shopping and bought everything I thought I wanted and some stuff that I didn't want or need. I took it anyway. She was a medical doctor who worked 12 and 14 hours a day. I didn't have to pay no bills. I would cook sometimes because she was not a good cook, but I didn't have to. I cooked for my benefit." I then asked, "There must be something she required of you?" He replied, "Yes, there are a few things. I must satisfy her sexually and that is not a problem for me. I have to take her to some social functions, and that's fine with me, too. I go on some trips with her and I really enjoy that. While she's taking care of business, I'm free to do whatever I want to do. That's about all I have to contribute. This gravy train ride is so smooth, all I can say is, how can I be so lucky?"

Marv, Your Majesty

The third criterion for the gravy train recipient is that he must believe that he is "All that." He will be placed on a pedestal by his keeper. In her mind, he is the top of the line. Well, her goal is to convince herself that he is a pot of gold. She lets him strut around *their house* like a gold guinea. Even though he moved into her house, she uses the language *our house* to him and to her friends.

I counseled a woman who let a male move in with her. Later, she told me that the man was a medical doctor, and he had owned a house in a posh neighborhood. He'd put an $80,000 down payment on the house and sold it for a million dollars. This was the story she told to everyone. It was not the truth. I have never understood why people pull out good Blue Cross Blue Shield cards, HAP, and hard-earned cash to sit on the other side of a desk in a therapy session that is set up to have them navigate through their problems with truth, and yet they choose to lie and lie and lie and lie. The third year into the therapy sessions, she tells the truth about the male she let move in with her. He was not a medical doctor, he was an elementary teacher. He did not live in a posh neighborhood; he lived in the inner city, in a neighborhood that was unkempt. He sold his house for $80,000, not a million dollars. When I asked her why she did not tell the truth in the beginning, her retort was, "I wanted people to think I really had a good catch." I replied, "There is nothing dishonorable about an elementary teacher who lived in a home that was worth less than $100,000." Her response was, "I know, but I just wanted my friends to see him as deserving of all the things I was doing for him." I then asked, "If you were trying to paint a picture to your friends and me that he was all that, why was it necessary to tell your friends all the things you were doing for him?" She responded, "I thought you and my friends may think I was justified in doing those things if he was looked upon as worthy of receiving them." At this point, all I could say was, "Okay!"

During a counseling session with a woman who had recently moved in her male companion, she mentioned that she and her son had an argument about the way she treated her live-in partner versus the way she treated him and his sister. He is 15 years old and his sister is 12. When asked about the content of the arguments, this is what she had to say. "My son is upset with me because I make my children eat after my boyfriend eats. He likes to eat by himself at the table and watch ESPN. He says that they make too much noise and he can't hear what they are saying on ESPN. So, they wait until after he's eaten. My son also complains about me waiting on my boyfriend. He says I treat my boyfriend like he is a kid and can't do anything for himself. I told him that when he gets grown and gets him a woman, he will want her to treat him like I treat my friend. Then he claims that since my friend moved in that I don't have any money anymore and that I don't do for them like I used to. I explained to them that they are older and don't need me to do what I used to do for them. He said that I buy more for my friend than I do for them. I told him, 'So what, it's my money. I work for it. And I can buy for anybody I want to buy for.' He kept on complaining about what I did for my man and what I didn't do for him and his sister, so I just told him that he didn't want me to have to make a choice." I asked, "Choice between whom?" She responded, "I meant that he had better not make me choose between them and my man." I posed this question, "If you had to make a choice between your two children and your man, who would you choose?" She replied, "I don't want to think about it. I love my man and I love my kids. Before I met him, I had been alone for a long time. [She stated that eight months was a long time.] I need a man. It's too hard to come home and not have anything to look forward to but your kids begging all the time." I asked, "You said that you buy gifts for your male friend." She replied, "Yeah, that's true, but he doesn't beg me to buy him anything like my children do. I just go out and get him what he needs or what he tells me he wants." At this point, I told her that at her next therapy session, I wanted her to tape herself and play the tape back, and at that time we would focus on what she thought of her comments. She never came to the next therapy session. I wonder why?

A Life Talk discussion on heterosexual cohabitation and the question of women allowing men to move in with them, especially if the men are unable to help out financially, was enthusiastically received. A male responded immediately to the question with the following thoughts. "Financial assistance isn't the only thing a man can contribute. I live with a woman and she treats me like a king. She's one of these desperate women. She has to have a man. She makes sure that I'm satisfied on all fronts. It's not my fault that she's desperate. If she didn't do the things for me, someone else would be in her house, getting all the gravy I get. So, I say if someone has to get it, why not me?"

Another male talked about his encounter with a woman who wanted him to move in. "I knew she wanted me to move in. I didn't really like her, but she was the best game in town at the time. She did everything for me but bow down at my feet. She got me out of debt. She bought me a van. And she gave me some money to pay the taxes on my property. I never had it so good. She gave me good sex every time I wanted it. Some of the stuff she did sexually didn't really do anything for me, but I let her go through her repertoire of sexual moves and grooves 'cause I knew that she would eventually get to some stuff that I liked—and she did. Don't get me wrong. I was holding my own with her in the bed. I don't think she had ever had good loving like I was putting on her. This woman thought more of me than I thought of myself. As a matter of fact, she thought more of me than my mother thinks of me, and I know that I'm the apple of my mother's eye. I wasn't about to go nowhere. When I would talk about her to my friends, all they would say is, 'Does she have a sister just like her?'"

It's obvious that these men have been "pedestalized" by the women with whom they are involved sexually. "Pedestalizing" a man refers to placing him far above and beyond a level than he can possibly reach. These men had no regrets regarding their newfound status. They thoroughly enjoyed being treated like crown jewels. The women appeared to have enjoyed pedestalizing these men, too. These women would make good teachers on the subject, *The "pedestalization" of a kept man.* I wonder how many women would be interested in such a class?

Female gravy trains are running constantly. Remember, every male cannot board these trains. If there were a female gravy train description of who qualifies to board these trains, it would probably read "No females allowed." Males must be willing and able to perform the following tasks:

- Ride the train for several years
- Provide good sex on a regular basis
- Provide companionship sometimes
- Participate in social activities outside the house—sometimes
- Accept gifts, both small and large
- Tell lies about how much he's in love
- Enjoy being "kept" by a woman
- Enjoy a woman waiting on you, hand and foot
- Enjoy being placed on a pedestal
- Enjoy being the number-one ranked person in your woman's life.

If you fit these qualifications, then *All Aboard!!!*

Fill out the survey below and find out if you fit this type of Player.

ARE YOU A GRAVY TRAIN PLAYER?

Directions: Answer the following questions honestly to find out if you are a Gravy Train Player. Circle the number by the answer that best describes you.

1) My woman lets me live with her for free.

1. Strongly Agree
2. Agree
3. Somewhat Agree
4. Disagree
5. Strongly Disagree

2) My woman will let me live with her as long as I want to.

1. Strongly Agree
2. Agree
3. Somewhat Agree

4. Disagree
5. Strongly Disagree

3) My woman has low self-esteem.

1. Strongly Agree
2. Agree
3. Somewhat Agree
4. Disagree
5. Strongly Disagree

4) My woman does everything I want her to do.

1. Strongly Agree
2. Agree
3. Somewhat Agree
4. Disagree
5. Strongly Disagree

5) My woman rarely if ever receives gifts from me.

1. Strongly Agree
2. Agree
3. Somewhat Agree
4. Disagree
5. Strongly Disagree

6) My woman is always buying gifts for me.

1. Strongly Agree
2. Agree
3. Somewhat Agree
4. Disagree
5. Strongly Disagree

7) My woman cooks for me.

1. Strongly Agree
2. Agree
3. Somewhat Agree
4. Disagree
5. Strongly Disagree

8) My woman cleans for me.

1. Strongly Agree
2. Agree
3. Somewhat Agree
4. Disagree
5. Strongly Disagree

9) My woman washes my clothes for me.

1. Strongly Agree
2. Agree
3. Somewhat Agree
4. Disagree
5. Strongly Disagree

10) My woman folds my clothes for me.

1. Strongly Agree
2. Agree

3. Somewhat Agree
4. Disagree
5. Strongly Disagree

11) My woman puts my clothes in the proper drawers for me.

1. Strongly Agree
2. Agree
3. Somewhat Agree
4. Disagree
5. Strongly Disagree

12) My woman chauffeurs me around.

1. Strongly Agree
2. Agree
3. Somewhat Agree
4. Disagree
5. Strongly Disagree

13) My woman has sex with me anytime I want it.

1. Strongly Agree
2. Agree
3. Somewhat Agree
4. Disagree
5. Strongly Disagree

14) My woman has sex with me anywhere I want it.

1. Strongly Agree
2. Agree
3. Somewhat Agree
4. Disagree
5. Strongly Disagree

15) My woman has sex with me any way I want it.

1. Strongly Agree
2. Agree
3. Somewhat Agree
4. Disagree
5. Strongly Disagree

16) My woman knows that if she doesn't cater to my needs the way I want her to, she will lose me.

1. Strongly Agree
2. Agree
3. Somewhat Agree
4. Disagree
5. Strongly Disagree

17) My woman ought to know that we have a noncommitted relationship.

1. Strongly Agree
2. Agree
3. Somewhat Agree
4. Disagree
5. Strongly Disagree

18) My woman lets me use her credit cards and/or she opens credit card accounts for me and pays the accounts.
1. Strongly Agree
2. Agree
3. Somewhat Agree
4. Disagree
5. Strongly Disagree

19) My woman will do almost anything to keep me.
1. Strongly Agree
2. Agree
3. Somewhat Agree
4. Disagree
5. Strongly Disagree

20) My woman will buy me anything I want if she has the money.
1. Strongly Agree
2. Agree
3. Somewhat Agree
4. Disagree
5. Strongly Disagree

Below are rating and scoring scales for males to complete to determine, by the rationale of these scales, if you are a Gravy Train Player category.

Rating Scale
Strongly agree = 5 points
Agree = 4 points
Somewhat agree = 3 points
Disagree = 2 points
Strongly Disagree = 1 point

Scoring Scale
90-100 = You are definitely a Gravy Train Player.
89-80 = You are a Gravy Train Player.
79-70 = You may be a Gravy Train Player.
69-60 = You are not a Gravy Train Player.
59 and below = You are definitely not a Gravy Train Player.

Below is a survey for women to determine if you are involved with a Gravy Train Player. See how you fit.

ARE YOU IN AN INTIMATE RELATIONSHIP WITH A GRAVY TRAIN PLAYER?

Directions: Answer the following questions honestly to find out if you are in an intimate sexual relationship. Circle the number by the answer that best describes you.

1) My man lives with me and doesn't pay any rent.
1. Strongly Agree
2. Agree
3. Somewhat Agree
4. Disagree
5. Strongly Disagree

2) My man can live with me as long as he wants to.
1. Strongly Agree
2. Agree
3. Somewhat Agree
4. Disagree
5. Strongly Disagree

3) I don't like to admit it, but my self-esteem is a little low.
1. Strongly Agree
2. Agree
3. Somewhat Agree
4. Disagree
5. Strongly Disagree

4) I do almost everything my man wants me to do.
1. Strongly Agree
2. Agree
3. Somewhat Agree
4. Disagree
5. Strongly Disagree

5) My man rarely gives me gifts.
1. Strongly Agree
2. Agree
3. Somewhat Agree
4. Disagree
5. Strongly Disagree

6) I'm always buying my man gifts.
1. Strongly Agree
2. Agree
3. Somewhat Agree
4. Disagree
5. Strongly Disagree

7) I cook for my man.
1. Strongly Agree
2. Agree
3. Somewhat Agree
4. Disagree
5. Strongly Disagree

8) I clean for my man.
1. Strongly Agree
2. Agree
3. Somewhat Agree
4. Disagree
5. Strongly Disagree

9) I wash my man's clothes.

1. Strongly Agree
2. Agree
3. Somewhat Agree
4. Disagree
5. Strongly Disagree

10) I fold my man's clothes.

1. Strongly Agree
2. Agree
3. Somewhat Agree
4. Disagree
5. Strongly Disagree

11) I put my man's clothes in the proper drawers.

1. Strongly Agree
2. Agree
3. Somewhat Agree
4. Disagree
5. Strongly Disagree

12) I chauffeur my man anywhere he wants to go, or I let him drive my car.

1. Strongly Agree
2. Agree
3. Somewhat Agree
4. Disagree
5. Strongly Disagree

13) I have sex with my man anytime he wants to.

1. Strongly Agree
2. Agree
3. Somewhat Agree
4. Disagree
5. Strongly Disagree

14) I have sex with my man any way he wants it.

1. Strongly Agree
2. Agree
3. Somewhat Agree
4. Disagree
5. Strongly Disagree

15) I have sex with my man anywhere he wants it.

1. Strongly Agree
2. Agree
3. Somewhat Agree
4. Disagree
5. Strongly Disagree

16) I know if I don't do all the things I do for my man, he will leave me.

1. Strongly Agree
2. Agree
3. Somewhat Agree

4. Disagree
5. Strongly Disagree

17) I know that this is a noncommitted relationship but I am trying to change his mind.

1. Strongly Agree
2. Agree
3. Somewhat Agree
4. Disagree
5. Strongly Disagree

18) I let my man use my credit cards and/or I open credit card accounts for my man and I pay for the accounts.

1. Strongly Agree
2. Agree
3. Somewhat Agree
4. Disagree
5. Strongly Disagree

19) I really, really want my man in my life.

1. Strongly Agree
2. Agree
3. Somewhat Agree
4. Disagree
5. Strongly Disagree

20) I will buy my man whatever he wants if I have the money.

1. Strongly Agree
2. Agree
3. Somewhat Agree
4. Disagree
5. Strongly Disagree

Below are the rating and scoring scales for you to see if you are in a relationship with a Gravy Train Player.

Rating Scale
Strongly Agree = 5 points
Agree = 4 points
Somewhat Agree = 3 points
Disagree = 2 points
Strongly Disagree = l point

Scoring Scale
90-100 = You are definitely with a Gravy Train Player.
89-80 = You are with a Gravy Train Player.
79-70 = You may be with a Gravy Train Player.
69-60 = You are not with a Gravy Train Player.
59 and below = You are definitely not with a Gravy Train Player.

Did you discover anything you didn't know about yourself and the man in your life? What, if anything, do you plan to do about your discovery? If you discover that you are in a relationship with a Gravy Train Player, the question is: Will you stay in it?

Chapter 2

The Mama's Boy Player

They call me a mama's boy
With an apron string around my neck
They claim I'm a lazy bum
And my life is a total wreck
I'm a chump so they say
As worthless as pebbles in the sand
I do what I do when I do it
Simply *because I can*

A man who mistreats his mother
Is who I really am
I make her cook and clean
Again, *because I can*
She washes and irons my clothes
Changes my bed sheets too
When my women call
She becomes my receptionist
She gladly takes my messages
Whether many or few

I am her male companion
Though we don't engage in sex
I'm as close as she will have to a husband
I'm all the love she's gonna get

Me, on the other hand,
I get lots of love
And my share of sex too
Women know their purpose in my life
Be available for sex
When I come to get it from you

My mama lets her boy live free
Since I first inhaled air
She spoiled me from the day I was born
Mistreating her is fair and square
The Making of the Personality of a Mama's Boy

I don't want to grow up, I'm a Toys R Us kid
There's a million toys at Toys R Us that I can play with!
From bikes, to trains, to video games,
It's the biggest toy store there is! Gee whiz!
I don't want to grow up, cuz baby if I did,
I wouldn't be a Toys R Us kid!

This Toys R Us jingle lays out a convincing rationale for the refusal of a kid to move from childhood to adulthood. It clearly makes known, without reservation, some of the many reasons that cause him to desire to remain a kid. 1) He wants to play and play and play with his toys. 2) He wants to pick and choose the toys with which he plays from a limitless collection. 3) He thoroughly enjoys his kid status. 4) He understands that as long as it's just him and his toys, he doesn't have to be responsible for carving out a productive and meaningful life for himself. 5) Finally, he knows that if he were to grow up, he would be forced to give up his never ending playtime with his toys. His ultimate goal is to have every toy he wants at his disposal for the rest of his life and, of course, remain a kid.

The characteristics of the kid described above illustrate just one aspect of a child's personality who could be well on its way to becoming a Mama's Boy. The key characteristic in a Mama's Boy, as expressed in the lyrics, is *I don't want to grow up*. Now the questions become: Who set him up to believe that he does not want to grow up? What factors led him to draw such a conclusion? And, how is this belief reinforced?

The following sections will explain other dimensions of a Mama's Boy and the role his mother plays in making him a dependent boy in a man's body.

According to Erik Erikson (as cited in Lindsey & Beach, 2000), a noted psychologist whose works were influenced by Sigmund Freud, asserted that early childhood experiences form the basis of one's personality. In addition, he developed eight stages of psychosocial development from infancy to adulthood. It was his position that everyone must go through these stages. For the purpose of this chapter, I have divided these stages into three types: Justifiable Total Dependency, Justifiable Selective Dependency, and Unjustifiable Dependency.

Justifiable Total Dependency
The Infancy Stage, 0-1 year old

Justifiable Selective Dependency
The Toddler Stage, 2-3 years old
Early Childhood, 3-5 years old

Unjustifiable Dependency
Elementary School, 6-12 years old
Adolescence, 13-19 years old
Young Adulthood, 20-40 years old
Middle Adulthood, 40-65 years old
Late Adulthood, 65 and over

Justifiable Total Dependency

Chapter 2: The Mama's Boy Player

Helpless, Egocentric, and Pleasure-Seeking: A Trilogy of Infancy Dependency

In the infancy stage, this bouncing baby boy is totally dependent on others to supply his physical and emotional needs. Because of his brief time in the world, he has not developed the emotional and cognitive wherewithal to be concerned about others. He wants what his biological drives tell him he wants. He has a right to be egocentric because his infancy stage of development means that his primary desires are dictated by what his body urges and child-driven selfishness tell him to desire. This causes him to respond positively to behavior that meets his needs and negatively to behavior that does not meet his needs, even when the latter behavior is for his own good. He acts as if he invented and holds the patent on the "I, me, and mine" mentality. After all, he doesn't have a clue as to the discomforts he is causing his caregiver. Since he is an infant and unaware of the needs of others, his selfishness not only makes sense, it is justified. This stage, as analyzed by Sigmund Freud, is id-driven. The *id,* from a Freudian point of view (as cited in Snowden, 2006), is the concept applied to that part of the self that houses the biological drives and human impulses. It is sometimes referred to as the *pleasure principle.* It is selfish, impulsive, spontaneous, self-serving, irrational, uncaring, and without a conscience. It seeks gratification and satisfaction at any cost and by any means necessary. This is why a baby cries when wet, hungry, too hot, too cold, or in pain, just to name few. This behavior in an infant is understood because the infant is without the knowledge and the maturity that affords him a considerate and altruistic attitude toward others. He can't help himself because he has only been on the face of earth a maximum of 12 months.

As later stages of development are discussed, remember what is included in this stage and why its inclusion makes sense in this stage and is ludicrous in the adulthood stage. The mother is usually the primary nurturer. The baby boy's basic necessities, such as food, clothing, shelter, love, and affection, are met in the form of feeding him, bathing him, changing his diapers, talking to him, singing to him, putting him to sleep, and making sure he is as comfortable as possible. She shows love and affection in the manner in which she holds him, the tone of voice and choice of words she speaks to him, and the symbols she uses to let him know that he is loved, wanted, and needed. The ties that bind the son to his mother are in full force.

One may be thinking by now, how does this mother's behavior toward her baby differ from behavior mothers have toward other male babies who will not become Mama's Boys and who are not female babies? In this stage, with the exception of two major factors that influence the development of a Mama's Boy, the behavior of all caring mothers is quite similar. The two exceptions are: 1) There is an exaggerated demonstration of love, care, attention, and affection she shows toward the future Mama's Boy, and 2) She is very possessive and overprotective of him. She intentionally attempts to keep others away from him, including his own father. She discourages others from attending to his needs under the guise that they don't know how to stop him from crying. They can't discern the meaning of different cries and what is required to fulfill the needs associated with them. Others cannot meet the need that has caused the baby boy to sob. They don't put his diaper on correctly. They don't hold him properly. They don't feed him at the right pace. They don't bathe him in the right amount of water, with the right temperature. They don't dry him with the right towel. They rub him too hard when drying him. And, they aren't gentle enough with him.

After the father, grandparents, aunts, uncles, and other primary group members hear these negative comments over time, they become reluctant to care for the baby. The enforcement of the *do not touch my baby boy* policy that was forced upon the baby's significant others by his mom exists for the sole purpose of discouraging others from caring for the baby. Since this is the stage in which the baby determines who to trust and who not to trust, the mother promotes a trusting bond between her and her baby boy and a distrusting detachment between her baby boy and others who are related to the baby boy by blood or marriage. The mother is fully aware that the trust foundation laid during infancy is expected to last for a lifetime. Therefore, the confidence bond is between the mother and the baby boy only. Mission accomplished! To further illustrate the seriousness of the mother's desire to separate her baby boy from others, one mother noted, "My boy doesn't need anyone but me in his life. I can teach him everything he needs to know." With cheers and pompoms waving, the end result of this mentality is that the mother celebrates her complete power, control, and domination over her precious baby boy.

Justifiable Selective Dependency
Who Am I?

Toddlers are mostly described as "the cutest little ones you will ever see" or "the terrible twos." Regardless of these descriptions, the basic personalities of these little ones are formed by two or three years of age. This means that set in this stage is the basic foundation of the baby boy's attitudes and behavior. His self-identity, social identity, sense of belongingness, and the behavior he exhibits with others are in their initial developmental phase and they are moving full throttle ahead. Yes, the personality of toddlers at two years old, in all likelihood, will show signs of who he will be at 20, 30, 40, and older. Charles Horton Cooley (1902) a noted sociologist, put forth a theory called The Looking Glass Self. At the base of this theory is the question, "Who Am I?" Cooley takes the position that significant others mirror who we are. Who relates to us and how they relate to us play key roles in the formation of personalities. The verbal and nonverbal communications used in the interaction are major determinants to how we will define ourselves. Cooley believes that our image of ourselves and our self-esteem are the result of our imagination of how others see us and our judgment of our perception of how they see us. Therefore, from this point of view, the making of the Mama's Boy is in the developing stage by the end of the toddler stage.

This stage can also be characterized by a tug-of-war between the establishment of self-control, learning to perform tasks on their own, and the development of a strong, positive self-esteem versus feelings of inadequacy, insecurity, and self-doubt.

When a mother encourages her son, provides him with constructive and consistent discipline, and promotes self-governance, her son, in all likelihood, will not become a Mama's Boy. On the contrary, when a mother promotes attitudes and behavior in her son that cause him to need her stamp of approval for virtually any of his thoughts or behavior, the making of a Mama's Boy is well on its way. Signs of lacking self-confidence, feelings of uncertainty, and decidophobia (a fear of making decisions) will become noticeable in the Mama's Boy as his dependency on his mother increases.

Early childhood is best described as the exploratory, inquisitive, and trial-and-error stage of development. Major goals to attain in this stage are to examine, explore, and investigate new behaviors and new ways of doing things. The parents, especially the mother, need to support this exploration and convince the child that he can achieve what he sets out to achieve.

Imagine if virtually every time a boy sets out to accomplish a task using new skills or a mixture of old and new skills, he is told that he cannot do it without his mother's help. Or, he is told that he is performing the tasks incorrectly. If this continues to happen, it could become a self-fulfilling prophecy. The self-fulfilling prophecy is a theory that asserts if a child is told something often, by his significant others, he will usually begin to believe it and act it out. For example, if the mother leads her son to believe that he is incapable of performing most tasks without her assistance, he will develop an excessive reliance on her to help him complete tasks or expect her to do all the work. Once this Mama's Boy mentality is established, the mother increases her power, control, and domination over her son. At this point, the baby boy's ties to his mother's apron strings are solidly in place. She has successfully convinced him that he cannot adequately function without her. At this point, the making of a Mama's Boy is in full swing.

Unjustifiable Dependency

Are We What Our Behavior Says We Are?

One of the most fascinating theories in the study of social behavior was put forth by Erving Goffman, a sociologist. The theory is known as the Dramaturgical Approach (as cited in Henslin, 2013). It combines the studies of sociology, drama, theater, and literature. Its major premise is that the world is a stage and we are all actors and actresses. It goes on to say that when we want to impress someone, we play the role of what Goffman calls "Impression Management", whereby we act out our most favorable side. He adds that in these social situations, we demonstrate our "Front stage behavior". "Impression Management" and "Front stage behavior" are used most frequently at job interviews and a first date with someone whom we really like.

In the case of the Mama's Boy, his goal is to satisfy his mother and behave in a way that impresses her. To achieve his goal, he uses "Impression Management" and "Front stage behavior" to satisfy his mother. Since she wants him to remain dependent on her for tasks that he is quite capable of performing for himself, she readily waits on him and does chores for him that he can do for himself. She may brush his teeth, dress him, make his bed, dust his room, run his bath water, put his shoes on, and tie his shoelaces. These gestures are designed to place doubt in the mind of the Mama's Boy about his ability to develop behavior that is independent of and equal to or better than that of his mother. Her goal is to get him to believe that he cannot exist in any positive and productive way without her.

As his primary nurturer and teacher, his mother socializes him to act, react, and respond to her and to others in ways that are pleasing to her. Therefore, a statement that best explains why he acts the way he acts is likely to be: As a Mama's Boy is taught how to act by his mother, so will he act. Now, the brainwashing for the successful implementation of unjustifiable dependency of the Mama's Boy toward his mother is well established. Between ages 6-12, this unnecessary dependency becomes full-blown. Under normal growth and maturation conditions, this stage would be characterized by the development of a sense of freedom and autonomy needed to accomplish tasks that were unattainable in previous stages. In addition, this stage is generally viewed as one of critical importance in the psychosocial developmental process. It is a time when males define themselves by their recognition or omission, successes or failures, assets or liabilities, strengths or weaknesses, and high self-esteem or low self-esteem. Because of the unnecessary influence of the mother on her Mama's Boy, unlike other males and females his age, his definition of who he is must be endorsed, sanctioned, and certified by his mother. In giving her son a definition of whom he is and disallowing him the right to define himself for himself, she perpetrates one of the greatest human frauds known to humanity. This fraud manifests itself in her telling everyone but her son that he can do no wrong. Then, she turns right around and tells her son that he can't do anything right unless she is orchestrating his moves.

He begins to rely on her for advice and guidance when it comes to the selection of friends, mates, social activities, and all other endeavors in which he is a participant. His mother is his *Dear Abby.* He literally develops emotional, psychological, and mental paralysis without his mother's input into almost every aspect of his life, regardless of how large or how small. This paralysis causes the Mama's Boy to doubt any independent thought he has. It is almost an everyday occurrence for him to say, "Let me check with my mother and see what she says."

As he moves from adolescence to young adulthood, to middle adulthood and to late adulthood, the paralysis and unjustifiable dependency intensifies. By now, he is so attached to his mother, he acts like she is still breast-feeding him. The dependency is quite visible in the manner in which she continues to indoctrinate him during his teenage years. The greater the indoctrination, the more he becomes less capable of seeing himself survive and prosper without her for the rest of his life. Although he says he's a man, he eats out of his mother's hand and fulfills her desires in almost every aspect of his life. With these dependency thoughts in the mind of the Mama's Boy toward his mother, she can make the following statement with conviction and assurance about the power and control she has over him: "I direct his path, I master his fate."

1+1+1=2: The Mama's Boys' Arithmetic

Mama's Boys are so attached to and dependent on their mothers that some of them tell their lady friends with whom they are in an intimate sexual relationship that their mother comes with the territory. Still others will let it be known that the mother's wishes and desires must be satisfied, even when the couple's plans conflict with the mother's demands on her son. In other words, women in the Mama's Boys' lives must understand that mothers come first! If the women don't like their rank order, the men quickly let them know that they can move on and find someone else. Yes, it is true that Mama's Boys practice a new arithmetic that is not taught in school. When it comes to their mothers and their female partners, they make it clear that 1+1+1=2. The first number one is the mother. The second number one is the mama's boy. The girlfriend's number doesn't even count.

Below are examples of Mama's Boy types and the women with whom they have come in contact. Remember females, they are who they are; they are not who you wish they were.

The Basement Brat

Imagine grown men in their '30s, '40s, and '50s living in their parents' basement for all or most of their adult life. This living arrangement is not a result of pursuing a college degree and saving money, layoffs or temporary unemployment. The biggest residential move Mama's Boys have ever made in their lives was from their bedroom on the first or second floor to the basement in their parents' home. They entertain their girlfriends, male friends, and engage in any social activity that suits their fancy in their parents' basement or anywhere they choose. In some cases, the parents let these Basement Brats have *sleepovers* with their girlfriends. By the way, they don't usually pay any rent. They don't pay utilities. And, they don't pay the telephone bill. They only pay their cell phone bill. It is not uncommon for these males to own a luxury car or an expensive SUV. In one case, the parents had three sons. One escaped the ravages of the mother's domination by enlisting in the military and marrying while overseas. To this end, you may ask, "What about the father? What was his role in this unjustifiable dependency?" In this case, the father sought out counseling in an attempt to figure out his role in stopping the growing dependency his sons had on their mother. In a therapy session, he stated that he complied with his wife's wishes to keep the peace; however, he admitted that it was becoming more than he could continue to take. An interesting part to this story is that both sons who lived in their home were gainfully employed. Both were capable of making financial contributions to the family's expenses but neither made an effort to do so. Whenever the father threatened to tell the sons they had to leave and find their own place, his wife would threaten to leave him. One son is 37 and other is 42 years old. The reason they do what they do is *simply because they can.*

Same Room Sunny Boy

Mama's Boys are often thought to always live with only their mothers. As noted in the Basement Brats, this is not the case. Fathers are in some of the homes with the Mama's Boys. Such is also the case of the Same Room Sunny Boy. This family has lived in their home for 52 years. The son, who happens to be an only child, has lived in the same house and in the same room all his life. The sizes of the beds were the major changes in his room. First, there was a crib. The crib was replaced by a baby bed. The baby bed was replaced with a twin bed. And the twin bed was replaced with a double bed. The same one-month-old baby boy, who slept in the crib, now occupies a double bed at 48 years of age. Same Room Sunny Boy admitted that his mother purchased each of the beds, without any financial help from him.

At a male-female relationship forum, a female raised the question about men who live at home. "Is it that they do not want the responsibility of taking care of a place of their own?" This male proudly stated that he has always lived at his parents' house and he has no plans to leave. Some asked if he stayed there because his parents were ill or because he was unemployed. He responded, "I have been employed for 29 years. I have four grown kids and I want them to come to a nice home to visit me, and since my parents have a nice big home, I don't see no reason why I need my own place." A male raised the question, "What do your grown kids think about their father who still lives with his parents?" Sunny Boy retorted, "Whenever that comes up in our conversation, I let them know that where I live is my business and not theirs."Another participant asked, "What happens when you are dating? Where do you entertain your female friends?" He replied, "At our house (referring to his parents' house). I have a key to the house and I come and go as I please." He went on and bragged about how he had the best of both worlds: "I have one foot in Sausalito and the other foot in Lake Tahoe; I have my mother who takes care of my nonsexual needs and some of my wants and my women take care of my sexual needs and wants away from home."

Codependent Companions: When Mother Knows Worst

Enablers are no strangers to codependent relationships. But when the relationship is between a mother and her son, it does take on a different twist from the type of relationship one may think of as being marred by enabling behavior. To complicate this even more, there may be a husband/father in the home. He and his wife rarely go out to dinner or social events. The mother uses her son to play the role of a surrogate nonsexual husband. It is obvious by now that the son has developed an indebtedness mentality toward his mother. Because of his history of dependency on her, he does not have the guts to tell her no, even when he has a date scheduled with his female friend. Moreover, he is afraid to defy the wishes of his mother because she will threaten to put him out or cut off his perks. The husband benefits from this surrogate-husband role played by the son because he doesn't want to be bothered with his wife at home. Nor is he interested in taking her out for a social event. When the Mama's Boy takes his mother out in the company of *her* girlfriends, he is required by his mother's law to dance with her 60-, 70-, and 80-year-old girlfriends. He takes their coats to the coatroom for coat check. He orders their drinks at the bar and uses the money his mother gave him to pay for their drinks. When the party is over, he is required, by his mother to get their coats. He must walk each of them to her car. In addition, he must meet all his mother's personal requests. This son is 54 years old. With the exception of the seven years he was married and lived with his wife and two kids some of that time, he has lived with his parents all his life. When asked how he copes with this type of mother-son relationship, he stated, "I get drunk and grin and bear it. I don't have a choice. If I act like I don't want to go along with my mother's wishes, she reminds me of all the things she does for me, such as letting me use her car, giving me money, allowing me to drink her liquor, and other things like washing my clothes or cleaning my room or cooking my meals. She's a good ol' girl most of the time, so I deal with it." The mother's benefit in keeping her son in a Mama's Boy role is seen in the way she is able to manipulate and control him. The mother is fully aware of her son's destructive drinking behavior, his irresponsibility toward manhood and adulthood, and his low self-esteem. The Mama's Boy also knows that his behavior is destructive. This exposé was given by the 54-year-old son in a classroom, in the midst of 47 students and visiting family members on a class day set aside for Family Day. Any member of the class or any family member taking part in Family Day has the right to respond to any comments. It was the overwhelming conclusion of the class participants that this male was crying out for help. The real tragedy, however, was that he probably will never seek professional counseling because of his fear of his own reality. Sometimes people ignore their reality because it is too intolerable.

The Lazy Leech

A 44-year-old single female came to me for therapy. She had three children, two girls and a boy, ages 12, 15, and 26, respectively. Her 26-year-old son dropped out of high school in the 10th grade. The mother claims that she can't get him to go back to school. He refuses to look for a job and he doesn't want to contribute to the household chores. She went on to say, "I clean his room because if I didn't, he wouldn't be able to get in it. I cook for him because I have to cook for my other kids and I buy his cigarettes. I don't want him to smoke but he has the habit so I try to help him deal with it." When I asked her if this son consumed any alcoholic beverages, she replied, "Yes, but I rarely buy him anything to drink." When I asked her if she thought she had any options to the way she was allowing her son to live off her, she quickly stated, "None that I know of. I can't put him out. He's my baby. Where would he go? His father is in prison so he can't help him. My family members will not help me because they say that I let him make a fool out of me. So, I'm at my wit's end." This 26-year-old bloodsucking parasite has been trained to live a nonproductive, irresponsible, and dysfunctional life at the expense of his mother. As long as she plays the role of an enabler, his self-destructive behavior, in all likelihood, will continue. By the way, in spite of his undesirable characteristics, his mother noted that he always has women in his life.

The Party Parasite

This Mama's Boy story has a spin to it that surprised almost everyone attending this male-female relationship class. During a discussion of males who become dependent on their mothers for a place to live and other basic necessities of life, a female asked to share a story about her mother and her brother with the class. She stated that her mother owns a 4,500-square-foot home. The mother allows her son to share the house with her. The sister stated that her brother has remodeled half of the house to suit him and his way of life. He converted two bedrooms into playrooms. These rooms have a billiard table, dart boards, a 60-inch flat screen television, and other miscellaneous toys for his entertainment. The sister says that about every two months, her brother has a party at the house. The mother prepares all the food for the party and leaves for the weekend so her baby boy and his friends can enjoy her house in her absence. When a member of the class asked how long this practice had been going on, the sister replied, "For the past three years." She went on to talk about how her mother told her that she had to get a job and pay rent while she was completing her college degree. She made it clear, according to the daughter that she could only be there for a year and after that, she needed to find her a place. "The hurtful part of all this was when I asked my mother why I couldn't stay longer than a year, she said because two grown women can't live in the same house and get along. I tried to explain that I would not get in her way, and she still told me, 'No!' I moved after six months into my own place. Except to visit for a couple of hours about once a week, I have not been back. My mother likes it that way. My brother likes it that way, and I do, too." In this scenario, three is one too many.

Do you remember the Toys R Us jingle at the beginning of the chapter? If it were transposed to fit the attitudes, behaviors, beliefs, and values of a Mama's Boy, the jingle may very well have these lyrics:

I don't want to grow up; I'm a Mama's Boy kid
There's a million things my mama does for me, my women could fulfill!
From cooking, to cleaning, to washing my clothes,
My women say my
Mama is the biggest fool there is! Gee whiz!
I don't want to grow up, cuz mama if I did
I wouldn't be your Mama's Boy kid!

Women, a surrogate mother's role may become available to you when the mother is too old and too tired to fulfill the needs of her Mama's Boy. Do you think you would like to apply?

Males, the survey below will allow you to rate and score yourselves to determine if you are Mama's Boys and the extent to which you fit this type of player.

ARE YOU A MAMA'S BOY PLAYER?

Directions: Answer the following questions honestly and discover if you are a Mama's Boy player. Circle the number by the answer that best describes you.

1) I live with my mother.
1. Strongly Agree
2. Agree
3. Somewhat Agree
4. Disagree
5. Strongly Disagree

2) I have no desire to leave my mother's house.
1. Strongly Agree
2. Agree
3. Somewhat Agree
4. Disagree
4. Strongly Disagree

3) I consider my mother's house to be my house.
1. Strongly Agree
2. Agree
3. Somewhat Agree
4. Disagree
5. Strongly Disagree

4) My mother cooks for me.
1. Strongly Agree
2. Agree
3. Somewhat Agree
4. Disagree
5. Strongly Disagree

5) My mother cleans for me.
1. Strongly Agree
2. Agree
3. Somewhat Agree
4. Disagree
5. Strongly Disagree

6) My mother changes the linen on my bed.
1. Strongly Agree
2. Agree
3. Somewhat Agree
4. Disagree
5. Strongly Disagree

7) My mother takes messages for me when my women call.
1. Strongly Agree
2. Agree
3. Somewhat Agree
4. Disagree
5. Strongly Disagree

8) I contribute little or nothing to help my mother maintain the house and pay the bills.
1. Strongly Agree
2. Agree

3. Somewhat Agree
4. Disagree
5. Strongly Disagree

9) I come and go as I please in my mother's house.

1. Strongly Agree
2. Agree
3. Somewhat Agree
4. Disagree
5. Strongly Disagree

10) My mother lets me mistreat her.

1. Strongly Agree
2. Agree
3. Somewhat Agree
4. Disagree
5. Strongly Disagree

11) My mother will let me live in her house until I die.

1. Strongly Agree
2. Agree
3. Somewhat Agree
4. Disagree
5. Strongly Disagree

12) My mother needs my male companionship.

1. Strongly Agree
2. Agree
3. Somewhat Agree
4. Disagree
5. Strongly Disagree

13) My mother treats me better than she treats her husband or better than she would treat a husband if she had one.

1. Strongly Agree
2. Agree
3. Somewhat Agree
4. Disagree
5. Strongly Disagree

14) The women with whom I have sex know that I will never leave my mother's house.

1. Strongly Agree
2. Agree
3. Somewhat Agree
4. Disagree
5. Strongly Disagree

15) The women with whom I am involved know that I'm only interested in a sexual relationship with them.

1. Strongly Agree
2. Agree
3. Somewhat Agree
4. Disagree

5. Strongly Disagree

16) I treat my mother the way I do because she lets me.

1. Strongly Agree
2. Agree
3. Somewhat Agree
4. Disagree
5. Strongly Disagree

17) I treat women with whom I have sexual relationships the way I do because they let me.

1. Strongly Agree
2. Agree
3. Somewhat Agree
4. Disagree
5. Strongly Disagree

18) I am the way I am because my mother spoiled me.

1. Strongly Agree
2. Agree
3. Somewhat Agree
4. Disagree
5. Strongly Disagree

19) It is my mother's fault that I'm no good for women who are looking for a good man.

1. Strongly Agree
2. Agree
3. Somewhat Agree
4. Disagree
5. Strongly Disagree

20) I don't have to grow up because my mother takes care of me.

1. Strongly Agree
2. Agree
3. Somewhat Agree
4. Disagree
5. Strongly Disagree

Below are the rating and scoring scales for you to determine if you are a Mama's Boy and how much of a Mama's Boy you are.

Rating Scale
Strongly agree = 5 points
Agree = 4 points
Somewhat agree = 3 points
Agree = 2 points
Strongly agree = 1 point

Scoring Scale
90-100 = You are definitely a Mama's Boy.

89-80 = You are a Mama's Boy.
79-70 = You may be a Mama's Boy.
69-60 = You are not a Mama's Boy.
59 and below = You are definitely not a Mama's Boy.

Now that you have rated and scored yourself, what do you think about your score? Do you think you need to change your behavior? Do you think you have the strength to change your behavior? Remember, no one has to know your score unless you want them to know it.

Women, below is your survey. Enjoy the process.

ARE YOU IN AN INTIMATE SEXUAL RELATIONSHIP WITH A MAMA'S BOY?

Directions: Answer the questions honestly and find out if you are dating a Mama's Boy player. Circle the number by the answer that best describes you.

1) My man lives with his mother.

1. Strongly Agree
2. Agree
3. Somewhat Agree
4. Disagree
5. Strongly Disagree

2) My man plans to continue to live at his mother's house.

1. Strongly Agree
2. Agree
3. Somewhat Agree
4. Disagree
5. Strongly Disagree

3) My man sees his mother's house as his house.

1. Strongly Agree
2. Agree
3. Somewhat Agree
4. Disagree
5. Strongly Disagree

4) My man's mother cooks for him.

1. Strongly Agree
2. Agree
3. Somewhat Agree
4. Disagree
5. Strongly Disagree

5) My man's mother cleans for him.

1. Strongly Agree
2. Agree

3. Somewhat Agree
4. Disagree
5. Strongly Disagree

6) My man's mother changes the linen on his bed.

1. Strongly Agree
2. Agree
3. Somewhat Agree
4. Disagree
5. Strongly Disagree

7) My man's mother takes messages for him when I call.

1. Strongly Agree
2. Agree
3. Somewhat Agree
4. Disagree
5. Strongly Disagree

8) My man contributes little or nothing to help his mother maintain the house and pay the bills.

1. Strongly Agree
2. Agree
3. Somewhat Agree
4. Disagree
5. Strongly Disagree

9) My man can come and go as he pleases in his mother's house.

1. Strongly Agree
2. Agree
3. Somewhat Agree
4. Disagree
5. Strongly Disagree

10) My man's mother needs his male companionship.

1. Strongly Agree
2. Agree
3. Somewhat Agree
4. Disagree
5. Strongly Disagree

11) My man's mother will let him live in her house until he dies.

1. Strongly Agree
2. Agree
3. Somewhat Agree
4. Disagree
5. Strongly Disagree

12) My man's mother lets him mistreat her.

1. Strongly Agree
2. Agree
3. Somewhat Agree

4. Disagree
5. Strongly Disagree

13) My man's mother treats him better than she treats her husband or better than she would treat a husband if she had one.

1. Strongly Agree
2. Agree
3. Somewhat Agree
4. Disagree
5. Strongly Disagree

14) I know that my man will never leave his mother's house.

1. Strongly Agree
2. Agree
3. Somewhat Agree
4. Disagree
5. Strongly Disagree

15) I know that my man is only interested in a sexual relationship with me.

1. Strongly Agree
2. Agree
3. Somewhat Agree
4. Disagree
5. Strongly Disagree

16) My man treats his mother the way he does because she lets him.

1. Strongly Agree
2. Agree
3. Somewhat Agree
4. Disagree
5. Strongly Disagree

17) My man treats me the way he does because I let him.

1. Strongly Agree
2. Agree
3. Somewhat Agree
4. Disagree
5. Strongly Disagree

18) My man is a spoiled boy.

1. Strongly Agree
2. Agree
3. Somewhat Agree
4. Disagree
5. Strongly Disagree

19) My man's mother is the reason he's no good for any woman.

1. Strongly Agree
2. Agree
3. Somewhat Agree
4. Disagree

5. Strongly Disagree

20) My man does not have to grow up because his mother takes care of him.

1. Strongly Agree
2. Agree
3. Somewhat Agree
4. Disagree
5. Strongly Disagree

Women, are you ready to rate and score yourselves? Your rating and scoring scales are below.

Rating Scale
Strongly Agree = 5 points
Agree = 4 points
Somewhat Agree = 3 points
Disagree = 2 points
Strongly Disagree = 1 point

Scoring Scale
90-100 = You are definitely dating a Mama's Boy.
89-90 = You are dating a Mama's Boy.
79-70 = You may be dating a Mama's Boy.
69-60 = You are not dating a Mama's Boy.
59 and below = You definitely are not dating a Mama's Boy.

Females, did you discover anything you didn't know? If so, what will you do about it? The choice is yours to make.

Mothers, it's your turn. Below is your survey. Reflect on the history of your relationship with your son and respond accordingly.

MOTHERS, DO YOU LET YOUR SON MISTREAT YOU?

Directions: Answer the following questions honestly. Circle the number by the answer that best describes you.

1) My son lives with me.

1. Strongly Agree
2. Agree
3. Somewhat Agree
4. Disagree
5. Strongly Disagree

2) My son has no desire to leave my home.

1. Strongly Agree
2. Agree

3. Somewhat Agree
4. Disagree
5. Strongly Disagree

3) My son acts like my house is his house.

1. Strongly Agree
2. Agree
3. Somewhat Agree
4. Disagree
5. Strongly Disagree

4) I cook for my son.

1. Strongly Agree
2. Agree
3. Somewhat Agree
4. Disagree
5. Strongly Disagree

5) I clean for my son.

1. Strongly Agree
2. Agree
3. Somewhat Agree
4. Disagree
5. Strongly Disagree

6) I change the sheets on the bed in which my son sleeps.

1. Strongly Agree
2. Agree
3. Somewhat Agree
4. Disagree
5. Strongly Disagree

7) I take telephone messages for my son.

1. Strongly Agree
2. Agree
3. Somewhat Agree
4. Disagree
5. Strongly Disagree

8) My son lives in my house for free.

1. Strongly Agree
2. Agree
3. Somewhat Agree
4. Disagree
5. Strongly Disagree

9) My son comes and goes as he pleases.

1. Strongly Agree
2. Agree
3. Somewhat Agree
4. Disagree
5. Strongly Disagree

10) I know my son takes advantage of me.
1. Strongly Agree
2. Agree
3. Somewhat Agree
4. Disagree
5. Strongly Disagree

11) My son can live in my house until he dies.
1. Strongly Agree
2. Agree
3. Somewhat Agree
4. Disagree
5. Strongly Disagree

12) I need my son for male companionship.
1. Strongly Agree
2. Agree
3. Somewhat Agree
4. Disagree
5. Strongly Disagree

13) For me, my son treats me better than my husband or better than having a husband.
1. Strongly Agree
2. Agree
3. Somewhat Agree
4. Disagree
5. Strongly Disagree

14) The women with whom my son is sexually involved know that he will never leave me.
1. Strongly Agree
2. Agree
3. Somewhat Agree
4. Disagree
5. Strongly Disagree

15) My son is only interested in a sexual relationship with the women with whom he is involved.

1. Strongly Agree
2. Agree
3. Somewhat Agree
4. Disagree
5. Strongly Disagree

16) My son treats me the way he does because I let him.
1. Strongly Agree
2. Agree
3. Somewhat Agree

4. Disagree
5. Strongly Disagree

17) My son treats the women with whom he is involved the way he does because he can.

1. Strongly Agree
2. Agree
3. Somewhat Agree
4. Disagree
5. Strongly Disagree

18) I know I spoiled my son.

1. Strongly Agree
2. Agree
3. Somewhat Agree
4. Disagree
5. Strongly Disagree

19) I know my son is no good for women who are looking for a good man because I didn't raise him to be a responsible man.

1. Strongly Agree
2. Agree
3. Somewhat Agree
4. Disagree
5. Strongly Disagree

20) My son doesn't have to grow up because I take care of him.

1. Strongly Agree
2. Agree
3. Somewhat Agree
4. Disagree
5. Strongly Disagree

The rating and scoring scales are below for you to attain your score.

Rating Scale
Strongly Agree = 5 points
Agree = 4 points
Somewhat Agree = 3 points
Disagree = 2 points
Strongly Disagree = 1 point

Scoring Scale
90-100 = You definitely fit this category.
89-80 = You fit this category.
79-70 = You somewhat fit this category.
69-60 = You do not fit this category.
59 and below = You definitely do not fit this category.

Mothers, how did you score? Do you think that you are the mother of a Mama's Boy? What was your role in the development of this type of male? If you are a mother who socialized her son into the Mama's Boy type, will you continue the same relationship you have with your son? If you are not the mother of a Mama's Boy, aren't you proud of yourself?

Chapter 3

The King Smorgasbord Player

I'm Mr. Delicious
I'm Mr. Delectable
I'm Mr. Yummy, yummy, yummy, yummy, yum
The women find me irresistible
They treat me like I'm their Kingdom come

I need many different women
All shapes, weights and heights
To satisfy my dried, candied and fleshy fruits
And savor my walnuts at night

I treat each one so special
While she is there with me
When she leaves, she's convinced
That she's the only woman I see

I could never be monogamous
So let the truth be known
Women love my pleasure driven lifestyle so much
Their dream is to see me cloned

Unforgettable—That's Who I Am

In the 1990s, Natalie Cole released an album entitled *Unforgettable… With Love,* featuring a duet with her father, Nat King Cole, singing the timeless song "Unforgettable." It was originally performed by her father in the 1950s. For more than 50 years, this song withstood the test of time. Four of the most amorous and meaningful lines in this song in conjunction with this chapter are: "Unforgettable, that's what you are… That's why, darling, it's incredible, that someone so unforgettable thinks that I am unforgettable, too." They are significant because a reciprocal "unforgettable experience" evolved between the two of them. He sees her as unforgettable and he is overwhelmed that she shares those sentiments toward him.

In spite of the romantic web that Nat King Cole weaved in this timeless melody, King Smorgasbord would never sing this song.

It is not in his purview to see any woman as unforgettable. To this end, Nat King Cole and King Smorgasbord are at opposite ends of the intimate relationship continuum. King Smorgasbord is no Nat King Cole and Nat King Cole was not and would not ever try to be a King Smorgasbord. If King Smorgasbord were to sing a song entitled "Unforgettable," the four significant lines might be: "Unforgettable, that's who I am... That's why, women, it's not surprising that you see me as so irresistible, and you know that I am the king of great loving, too." He not only sees himself as unforgettable, he may compile a list of adjectives to describe his loving and lovable qualities. They will probably bear the title and adjectives below.

10 Reasons Why Women Find Me Unforgettable

I AM:

1. *Luscious*
2. *Delectable*
3. *Adorable*
4. *Scrumptious*
5. *Delicious*
6. *Pleasing*
7. *Enjoyable*
8. *Pleasurable*
9. *Gratifying*
10. *Appetizing*

For the doubters of his charm and sexual prowess, he will simply say, "Follow me home and sample me for yourself." He's the type to tell women that a sample of him will only make them mad, miserable, moody, and in dire need of a full-course sexual meal from him. At this point, the obvious is noticeably clear. King Smorgasbord is one of the most braggadocious players. He is quick to use phrases like, "There's no shame to my game." His own personal belief is "I am the universe's gift to women." He is so full of himself, his more extensive definition of who he is may take on these expressions:

Self-confidence, I have it.

Self-worth, I waddle in it.

Self-admiration, I bathe in it.

Self-centeredness, I'm draped in it.

Self-assuredness, I wear it.

Self-assertiveness, I move by it.

Self-conceitedness, I speak on it.

These men have such a high opinion of themselves, they fervently believe that they can turn a woman on sexually better than any other man.

Whosoever Will, Let Her Come and Come and Come Some More

When it comes to women, King Smorgasbord is probably one of the most nondiscriminating players. His taste buds in women go from sweet or sour, to spicy or bland, to juicy or dry, to soft or hard, to fluffy or flat, to tangy or tart, and to hot or cold. When it comes to women's attitudes and demeanor, King Smorgasbord will take:

The meek and mild,

The loud and boisterous,

The rude and obnoxious,

The timid and submissive,

The outspoken and loquacious,

The funny and hilarious,

The serious and earnest,

The trusting and trustworthy,

The outrageous and scandalous,

The moral and ethical,

The loose and immoral,

The friendly and gregarious,

The lovable and adorable,

The offensive and hostile.

His appetite for women is so huge, he doesn't care if they epitomize every concept of beauty associated with women or resemble the most unattractive women to ever grace Earth. He accepts all of them without hesitation. Regardless of whether they are young or old, petite or overweight, pale or tan, short or tall, sexy or plain, he probably will not classify any as rejects.

In a For Males Only Life Talk class with a group of 16 men ranging in age from 22 to 47, a discussion on the type of women they preferred dominated the discourse. The central prompt was: Describe the type of women you prefer and explain why you have this preference. Nine of the 16 stated that their only preference was that "she's a woman." As one of the nine stated, "If she has a vagina, she'll do." The discussion then moved to the meaning of prejudice and discrimination in the selection of women in intimate sexual relationships. In this context, it was explained that prejudice is an attitude in favor of or against women. Discrimination, on the other hand, is a behavior that acts out negative attitudes toward women. The need for prejudicial attitudes and discriminatory behavior was associated with those same needs in the selection and consumption of foods. The following points were noted by the facilitator. "The two encounters that are most deserving of and have a strong justification for prejudice and discrimination are food consumption and mate selection. The closest a person will get to you is in sexual relationships. When bodies intertwine and sexual activities take place, each partner potentially can be exposed to any transmittable disease living in the body of the other. Therefore, if ever there is a legitimate reason to discriminate, it is when a person is choosing a sexual partner."

One of the males stated, "Do you think that men ask about diseases before they screw a woman? You act like people are going to carry around a clean bill of health card that says whether they are clean or dirty." The facilitator retorted, "No, I don't think that. First of all, a good health card on a Monday could be a bad health card on Tuesday, if the health card carrier has engaged in sex with someone who has an STD (sexually transmitted disease), HIV/AIDS, or herpes, and has contracted the disease. Since the card will not reflect that because it has not been updated, the sex partner will not know of the danger that may be staring him or her in the face."

The facilitator continued this line of thought and shared an exchange that occurred in a therapy session with a female who was concerned as to whether or not she had contracted an STD, HIV/AIDS, or herpes from a male she had recently met and dated twice. The female asked the therapist about the most foolproof method she could use to protect herself prior to having sex with him when the time was right. The therapist suggested that she ask her mate if he would agree to go with her to a physician and the two of them undergo STD, HIV/AIDS, and herpes blood work to determine if either had contracted one of the diseases. When she returned for her next therapy session, she shared with me her mate's response to my suggestion. In her own words, she said, "He first told me that he goes to the doctor all the time and he was clean. I asked him when was the last time he was tested for STDs, HIV/AIDS, or herpes, and he said he didn't remember but he knew he was 'clean'. I asked him how he knew he was 'clean'. He responded, 'I just know.' He told me that he was disappointed with me and my distrust of him, and he flatly refused to go to the doctor with me. He even went so far as to say that I must be out of my mind to ask him something like that. He said that it only proved to him that I didn't trust him. The last straw was when he told me that if I wanted him to go with me to be tested, I needed to find a chump, and that he was a man, from head to toe. I like this man. I really like him. What should I do?"

Men who have just read this know what the man is saying and why he is saying it. Men understand that most women believe most of what men say. Consequently, men will say what they think a woman wants to hear or what is in their best interest. In the case of the conversation at the doctor's office, the male's response was to hopefully intimidate the woman in a way that would cause her to refrain from asking him about being tested for a second, third, or fourth time, and settle for whatever explanation he gave her. The concept I coined to label this behavior is Mr. Triple Bs—the *Bold, Barefaced Bully.* Mr. Triple Bs is a man who is fearless, unafraid, nervy, shameless, brassy, brazen, and intimidating. By the way, he offers no apology for his affect, mood, or behavior. Below are some King Smorgasbord Player types with traits of Mr. Triple Bs. See if you recognize any of them, up close and personal or from a distance.

Delectable Dan

A 56-year-old woman made a startling admission in a therapy session regarding the 35-year-old man with whom she was engaged in a sexual relationship. "He's what I want but he is not what I need. I have tried to stop seeing him but I keep going back to him. I just can't resist him. It's like I'm hypnotized by him. I know my man is involved with other women because he tells me. I also know because sometimes he can't perform sexually or he can only last for about three minutes. I know that he can give me an STD but I continue to see him as if nothing bad will happen to me. From the woman's point of view, he was Delectable Dan.

The above confession is just one example that explains how and why women react to Delectable Dan and why they find him sexually delicious. If it doesn't give a clear picture of the effects Delectable Dans have on women, then imagine having your favorite food that you are not supposed to eat, prepared to perfection. You know you need to resist it but you don't have the willpower and self-control to refrain from consuming it. So you indulge, knowing that you will have a tremendous price to pay. Since you are out of control, you can't wait to eat it. Second, as you eat, you savor every bite as if you are prolonging the inevitable—the end of the meal. As you finish, you adopt a popular phrase and with conviction you say, "Good to the very last drop." Plain and simple, the women see Delectable Dan as delicious, scrumptious, and yummy, yummy, yummy, yummy, yum.

Ernie the Entitled

"I am the moral authority. I have a right to have any woman I want whenever I want her. I have as much right to do what I want to do simply because I want to do it." He really thinks that when it comes to women, he is a god to them. This point of view was expressed by a male hairstylist who was in therapy to determine what he needed to do to get his son to value education. His son had dropped out of high school in the 10th grade and was living a street life. This man was his biological father but the son was living with his mother. He admitted that he had not had a consistent relationship with his son. The mother had called him seeking his help in getting their son on the right track. I gave him my article entitled "The Street Definition of Masculinity Breeds Lawlessness." I requested that he give a copy of the article to his son and discuss the article with his son to get a better understanding of his son's definition of himself, his value or devaluation of education, and his goals for the future.

As the sessions continued, it became clear that the father needed therapy about some of his issues of manhood, masculinity, and fatherhood. The later sessions focused on the father's relationship with women and his definition of who he was in relationship to his son, his son's mother, and women in general. The father admitted that he saw himself as the master of everything with which he came in contact and virtually every woman he thought he wanted. He noted that when it came to women, he felt that he should have any woman he desired. In his own words, he acknowledged, "I thought I had to have sex with every woman whose hair I styled. They must have agreed with me since only two of them turned me down. Married, single, living with somebody, it didn't matter because they let me have my way. I felt that since they didn't object to my advances, I was entitled to have them."

This type of attitude toward women and sex epitomizes an entitlement mentality. As he discussed his sexual escapades with women, he would chuckle in between the stories. When I asked him what was funny, he responded, "Me, men—you know, we [men] are amused by our own behavior, no matter how scandalous women or society may see it." It was obvious that he really enjoyed talking about women, how he conquered them sexually, and their reactions to his sexual conquests. I also asked, "How do you feel after your sexual accomplishments?" He retorted, "How do I feel? I don't have no sympathy for the women, if that's what you mean. I didn't promise them nothing but sex, and that's what they got and they enjoyed it." I then replied, "Does your conscience ever bother you about your indiscriminate sex life?" He responded, "No, why should it*? The penis has no conscience."* It is interesting how this man detached his penis from himself and acted as if it was not his fault that the penis did what it did with whom it did it. It was as if he was saying that the penis knows no right or wrong, good or evil, loyalty or disloyalty, and honor or dishonor. When asked who would be responsible if he slapped someone or stepped on someone's foot or elbowed someone, he did not hesitate to say he would be responsible. Continuing my inquiry, I said, "If you are responsible for the movements of your feet, hand, and elbow, why aren't you responsible for the actions of your penis?" He responded, "I never thought about it like that." What was most interesting is how this man used a different logic to explain the movements of his penis versus the movements of other parts of his body. When the discussion regarding the behavior of his penis was revisited, he stated in a cavalier way, "If women don't like the way I use my penis, it's up to them to change their ways. Since I'm not a rapist, I can only have sex with women who allow me to. If they want to stop me from having sex with them, they need to stop making it so available."

Women, the hairstylist has spoken. Change your sexual behavior and penises will change theirs. They will have no other choice.

Greedy Greg

If Greedy Greg were told to play a word-association game using the word *women* over and over again, reciting the first word that comes to his mind, he would probably say the following: variety, abundance, many, plenty, diversity, bonanza, bunch, heap, and quantity. He truly believes in a non-discriminatory platform when it comes to women. Although kings are usually associated with queens, King Smorgasbord defies that association. For him, any woman will do. He doesn't care if she is unemployed, underemployed, works part-time, sometimes, full-time, overtime, double time, or triple time, he will take her. He doesn't care if she has an MD, PhD, EdD, JD, DDS, or "noD" at all, she is prime stock for him. He doesn't care if she is a queen, princess, maid, nanny, babysitter, or homeless, he will have sex with her. Greedy Greg likes women of any shape, height, weight, class, and size. She can wear a size 0 or a size 22; he will make himself available to her. She can stand 4 feet or 6 feet; she will not be too short or too tall for him. She can weigh 70 or 350 pounds; she will not be too small or too large for him. He is to women what a greedy man is to food; he likes them all, just like a man who is greedy for food likes the appetizer, entree, sides, salad, soup, beverage, and dessert. Greedy Greg considers himself the king of the *random acts of knocking boots.*

At an informal gathering with seven men and four women, the men began talking about the different type of women they had met and those with whom they had sex. One male asked the other males, "Man, have you ever had sex with a stinky woman?" They shouted a unanimous yes. He went on to talk about a night when he was at a club and met this woman. "Man, she was fine. Her hair was beautifully cut and styled. Her nails were well manicured, and her clothes were of the latest fashion. They fitted her like they were custom made for her. As I talked to her, she was witty, she sounded intelligent, and she was easy to talk to. She could dance and she felt so good when I danced with her. I asked her if she had any plans after she left the club and she said, no. I suggested that we go to my place and have a drink or two. She suggested her place. That was fine with me. When we arrived at her place, we had a drink and I suggested we watch a movie. The television was in her bedroom. We started out lying down on top of the comforter. Then the foreplay was on. I helped her take off her clothes. She took over and started to take off my clothes. I turned out the lights and it's a good thing I did. By the time I had turned out the lights, she was under the sheets. I continued with the foreplay. I made a mistake and raised the sheets up and my nose went slightly under them. This well-groomed woman had the worst odor I had ever smelled on a woman in my life." One of the women asked, "So what did you do?" He responded, "Well, I had gotten that far, I decided that I might as well try to hold my nose and take care of business. She may have been funky, but the sex was good."

The discussion then shifted to having sex with fat and obese women. One man testified that a fat woman wanted to get with him. He went on to talk about how he thought he was having sexual intercourse with her. "Man, I was just stroking and stroking and she was moaning and groaning. I looked down and realized that I was screwing her in one of those creases on her thigh." One of the other men asked, "What did you do?" He responded, "I had gone that far, I figured I might as well keep stroking and come back the second time and get the real thing." The men had a hearty laugh and almost in unison, they chanted phrases that supported the man's sexual behavior with the overweight woman. This is just another example of how a Smorgasbord Player relates to women.

It is no secret that men enjoy talking about sports and politics with other men. Their favorite team, their favorite players, great players, lousy players, who will win the championship, how much money players make and those who deserve and don't deserve their salaries are just some of the topics that dominate their discussions. Women and sex are often major subjects men love to discuss, too. It is not uncommon to find a group of men at a bar, a club, or an informal gathering, laughing and bragging about their sexual conquests. These conversations are almost always *for men only.* If a woman is allowed to be in their presence during these discussions, you can guarantee that she is not one of the men's wives, unmarried significant other, or one of his sex partners. If a woman is in their midst, she is a platonic friend or a person who is gathering data on the subject. The latter is fine with them because it raises their sense of importance. They see themselves as having knowledge that is worthy of recording and putting in print. Under these circumstances, they will talk, and talk, and talk. Such was the case in the situation cited above.

At a well-known club, men were sitting around the bar, drinking their favorite beverage, and the subject of women and sex came up. It was interesting to see how the body language of the men changed. They smiled, laughed, interrupted each other, and waved their arms as if to say "I got next to tell my story." These men knew me, as I had held a focus group with some of them in attendance. At the focus group, I read some of my poems to get their reaction. Because of that experience and the fact they knew I was writing a book on men, I became "one of the boys." This club attracts men from all walks of life, from judges, lawyers, medical doctors, dentists, teachers, owners of car dealerships, real estate brokers, skilled tradesmen, and production workers, just to name a few. The club is also known for its delicious cuisine. One of the men had ordered a dinner. When it arrived, one of the men began to tease one of the other men, telling him that every time he sees him, he is eating. The man continued by saying that he had never seen the guy eat the same food. The man about whom he was referring responded, "That's because I like my food the way I like my women and the ways I like to have sex with my women. I don't like the same type women all the time, just like I don't like to eat the same food all the time. I like different food prepared in different ways, just like I like my women. That's why I come here to eat." Another one of the men said, "So how do you like your women and how do you like to have sex with your women?" The man replied, "I like 'em deep fried, boiled, broiled, baked, and roasted. You name it, I like it." The other men were laughing and holding sidebar conversations between themselves. Later, one of the other men said, "Hey, I know what you mean because I like a variety of women, too." As the conversation continued, the men chimed in and began to associate different ways food is prepared with different women and the different ways to have sex. The men began to use analogies of women and sex to food. One by one, they chanted: "I like my women and my sex…

Raw

Shake and bake

Well done

Steamed

Smothered

Medium rare

Pan fried

Flame broiled

Sautéed

Barbequed

and

Over easy"

As the men "roll called" their associations of food with women, they laughed, gave each other high-fives and slapped each other on the back. They were thoroughly enjoying this exchange. As I set there, laughing too, I thought to myself, women need to be exposed to this type of conversation.

In another conversation with men and their desire to have a variety of women, one man said that the selection of women is like going to a Baskin-Robbins Ice Cream Parlor. "They advertise 31 flavors and you like them all. So you find yourself saying that the double fudge is pretty good, but so is the butter pecan, and the vanilla, and the chocolate, and the pralines 'n cream. Even though I really want to sample all 31 flavors, I settle for a few different ones at a time and tell myself that two or three flavors will do for now."

These examples demonstrate the true meaning of a King Smorgasbord's mentality and his language. It also exposes one of the levels of amusement men experience when talking about women and sex. Beware, women! You may be to a man what food preparations are to a chef—*just a different way to show off his sexual culinary skills.*

Men, how would you like to test your sexual greed? Here is your opportunity. Fill out the survey and see what it reveals.

ARE YOU A KING SMORGASBORD PLAYER?

Answer the following questions honestly and find out if you are a King Smorgasbord Player. Circle the number by the answer that best fits you.

1) I am irresistible to women.

1. Strongly Agree

2. Agree

3. Somewhat Agree

4. Disagree

5. Strongly Disagree

2) I like many different women.

1. Strongly Agree

2. Agree

3. Somewhat Agree

4. Disagree

5. Strongly Disagree

3) I need to have relationships with two or more women at the same time.

1. Strongly Agree

2. Agree

3. Somewhat Agree

4. Disagree

5. Strongly Disagree

4) I am a pleasure seeking man.

1. Strongly Agree

2. Agree

3. Somewhat Agree

4. Disagree

5. Strongly Disagree

5) I like women of all shapes and weights.

1. Strongly Agree

2. Agree

3. Somewhat Agree

4. Disagree

5. Strongly Disagree

6) I treat each one of my women special so they can think that they are the only woman in my life.

1. Strongly Agree

2. Agree

3. Somewhat Agree

4. Disagree

5. Strongly Disagree

7) I desire to get all the sexual satisfaction I can get from these women.

1. Strongly Agree

2. Agrcc

3. Somewhat Agree

4. Disagree

5. Strongly Disagree

8) I have a huge sexual appetite.

1. Strongly Agree

2. Agree

3. Somewhat Agree

4. Disagree

5. Strongly Disagree

9) I need a lot of emotional attachment from women.

1. Strongly Agree

2. Agree

3. Somewhat Agree

4. Disagree

5. Strongly Disagree

10) I have many sexual wants that women must satisfy.

1. Strongly Agree

2. Agree

3. Somewhat Agree

4. Disagree

5. Strongly Disagree

11) I have many sexual needs that women must satisfy.

1. Strongly Agree

2. Agree

3. Somewhat Agree

4. Disagree

5. Strongly Disagree

12) I have many sexual desires that women must satisfy.

1. Strongly Agree

2. Agree

3. Somewhat Agree

4. Disagree

5. Strongly Disagree

13) I like women to make me feel good sexually.

1. Strongly Agree

2. Agree

3. Somewhat Agree

4. Disagree

5. Strongly Disagree

14) I like women of all different heights.

1. Strongly Agree

2. Agree

3. Somewhat Agree

4. Disagree

5. Strongly Disagree

15) I know that I am the best thing that ever happened to the women with whom I am sexually involved.

1. Strongly Agree

2. Agree

3. Somewhat Agree

4. Disagree

5. Strongly Disagree

16) I like to control my women.

1. Strongly Agree

2. Agree

3. Somewhat Agree

4. Disagree

5. Strongly Disagree

17) I like to rule my women.

1. Strongly Agree

2. Agree

3. Somewhat Agree

4. Disagree

5. Strongly Disagree

18) I like to dominate my women.

1. Strongly Agree

2. Agree

3. Somewhat Agree

4. Disagree

5. Strongly Disagree

19) I demand genuine affection from my women.

1. Strongly Agree

2. Agree

3. Somewhat Agree

4. Disagree

5. Strongly Disagree

20) My women must be available when I need or want them for sexual pleasures.
1. Strongly Agree

2. Agree

3. Somewhat Agree

4. Disagree

5. Strongly Disagree

Below are the rating and scoring scales to determine if you are a King Smorgasbord and the degree to which you fit this type player. It will also tell you if you are not a King Smorgasbord Player.

Rating Scale

Strongly Agree = 5 points

Agree = 4 points

Somewhat Agree = 3 points

Disagree = 2 points

Strongly Disagree = l point

Scoring Scale

90-100 = You are definitely a Smorgasbord Player.

89-80 = You are a Smorgasbord Player.

79-70 = You could be a Smorgasbord Player.

69-60 = You are not a Smorgasbord Player.

59 and below = You are definitely not a Smorgasbord Player.

Now that you have completed the survey and tabulated your score, how greedy is your sexual appetite?

Women, it is now your turn. Did you ever wonder if the man with whom you are involved has an insatiable sexual appetite? Fill out the survey below and find out.

ARE YOU IN AN INTIMATE SEXUAL RELATIONSHIP WITH A KING SMORGASBORD PLAYER?

Directions: Answer the following questions honestly and find out if you are in an intimate sexual relationship with a King Smorgasbord Player. Circle the number by the answer that best fits you.

1) My man is just irresistible to me.

1. Strongly Agree
2. Agree
3. Somewhat Agree
4. Disagree
5. Strongly Disagree

2) My man likes many different women.

1. Strongly Agree
2. Agree
3. Somewhat Agree
4. Disagree
5. Strongly Disagree

3) My man needs to have a relationship with two or more women at the same time.

1. Strongly Agree

2. Agree

3. Somewhat Agree

4. Disagree

5. Strongly Disagree

4) My man seeks pleasure and pleasure only.

1. Strongly Agree

2. Agree

3. Somewhat Agree

4. Disagree

5. Strongly Disagree

5) My man likes women of all shapes and weights.

1. Strongly Agree

2. Agree

3. Somewhat Agree

4. Disagree

5. Strongly Disagree

6) My man treats me special because he wants me to think that I am the only woman with whom he is in a relationship.

1. Strongly Agree

2. Agree

3. Somewhat Agree

4. Disagree

5. Strongly Disagree

7) My man believes in getting all the sexual satisfaction he can get from every woman.

1. Strongly Agree

2. Agree

3. Somewhat Agree

4. Disagree

5. Strongly Disagree

8) My man has a huge sexual appetite.

1. Strongly Agree

2. Agree

3. Somewhat Agree

4. Disagree

5. Strongly Disagree

9) My man needs a lot of emotional attachment from the women with whom he is involved.

1. Strongly Agree

2. Agree

3. Somewhat Agree

4. Disagree

5. Strongly Disagree

10) My man wants me and other women to satisfy his many sexual wants.

1. Strongly Agree

2. Agree

3. Somewhat Agree

4. Disagree

5. Strongly Disagree

11) My man wants me and other women to satisfy his many needs.

1. Strongly Agree

2. Agree

3. Somewhat Agree

4. Disagree

5. Strongly Disagree

12) My man wants me and other women to satisfy his many desires.

1. Strongly Agree

2. Agree

3. Somewhat Agree

4. Disagree

5. Strongly Disagree

13) My man loves for me to make him feel good.

1. Strongly Agree

2. Agree

3. Somewhat Agree

4. Disagree

5. Strongly Disagree

14) My man likes women of different heights.

1. Strongly Agree

2. Agree

3. Somewhat Agree

4. Disagree

5. Strongly Disagree

15) I know my man is the best thing that ever happened to me.

1. Strongly Agree

2. Agree

3. Somewhat Agree

4. Disagree

5. Strongly Disagree

16) My man likes to rule me.

1. Strongly Agree

2. Agree

3. Somewhat Agree

4. Disagree

5. Strongly Disagree

17) My man likes to control me.

1. Strongly Agree

2. Agree

3. Somewhat Agree

4. Disagree

5. Strongly Disagree

18) My man likes to dominate me.

1. Strongly Agree

2. Agree

3. Somewhat Agree

4. Disagree

5. Strongly Disagree

19) My man demands genuine affection from me.

1. Strongly Agree

2. Agree

3. Somewhat Agree

4. Disagree

5. Strongly Disagree

20) I am available whenever my man needs me or wants me.

1. Strongly Agree

2. Agree

3. Somewhat Agree

4. Disagree

5. Strongly Disagree

Below are the rating and scoring scales for you to determine if you are in a relationship with a King Smorgasbord Player.

Rating Scale

Strongly Agree = 5 points

Agree = 4 points

Somewhat Agree = 3 points

Disagree = 2 points

Strongly Disagree = 1 point

Scoring Scale

90-100 = You are definitely in a relationship with a King Smorgasbord Player.

89-80 = You are in a relationship with a King Smorgasbord Player.

79-70 = You may be in a relationship with a King Smorgasbord Player.

69-60 = You are not in a relationship with a King Smorgasbord Player.

59 and below = You are definitely not in a relationship with a King Smorgasbord Player.

Is your mate guided by sexual greed or is he not? No one has to know the answer

to the question but you.

Chapter 4

The Gas and Go Player

I gas up and fill up
My sexual libido tank
I don't want unleaded or mid-grade
Premium only meets my rank

That part of a woman's body
Located about 9 inches below the naval
And 14 inches above the knees
Is the only part I'm interested in
It's the only part I want and need

She's known as my booty call
Though she may not admit it
She thinks she's got it going on
When I'm only interested in
What's between her legs
And maybe-sometimes her titties

Yes, I act like Houdini
With sexual tricks up my sleeve
I pull out my hypnotic white dove
I let her sex me
Until I'm ready to leave

I come when I get ready
I go when I please
There is nothing she can do about that
Now you see me
Now you don't
Just fulfill my sexual needs
And my sexual wants

She thinks I like and love her
That's the lie she tells herself
I am the sex mobile in her life
She's always horny for me
And sexually ripe

DON'T HATE THE PLAYER LEARN THE GAME

My woman is a high octane woman
Producing forceful and intense sex
She uses her energized sex machine
To keep me from making her my ex

I don't care if her high voltage sex engine
Performs better than the best V8
I'll still be her gas and go man
When I need to park my engine
At her welcome home gate

A Sketch of a Male Sex Mobile

"A man is like water. He takes the path of least resistance." This statement was made by a man in his '40s at a male-female relationship forum for singles. It was in response to a female's comment about the difficulty in finding men who were interested in developing meaningful, long-lasting relationships. What followed was a chorus of chants from men using phrases that co-signed the above quote. These phrases took the form of, "Y'all women want us [men] to wine and dine you and spend money on you. Yeah, women want men to sit with them and take them out dancing and listen to their problems. We men don't have time for that kind of stuff. We just want to get the relationship going." When the man was asked by one of the female participants to explain what he meant by "get the relationship going," his retort was, "You know, go on and have sex."

Another woman raised the question, "Whatever happened to getting to know each other?" The male replied, "We already know enough about each other. We know that you are females and we are males. That's enough. Women need to understand that just because they may only want one man in their lives doesn't mean that men only want one woman in their lives. Maybe men need more than one woman to satisfy all our sexual needs." A different male added, "That's right! I know that one woman is not enough for me. One woman has never been enough for me. And, I don't think one woman will ever be enough for me. You got all these beautiful women. Look around this room at all these beautiful women. It's hard to settle for just one of you. It's just too much temptation. I just can't resist all these women and I guess they can't resist me, 'cause I couldn't have more than one woman if they didn't want me."

As the facilitator, I explained to the men that their points of view were well taken; however, "the title of the forum was Friends First for the purpose of emphasizing the need for potential couples to get to know each other before sex occurs." A male immediately raised his hand to express his disagreement with the facilitator's statement: "When I meet a woman, I'm not looking for a woman to marry or a woman to have my children. I'm looking for someone to have fun with. I don't have to know someone to have sex with them and they don't have to know me. All that getting to know you stuff is for men who want to settle down and have a family, and that ain't me."

In response to these statements, a woman begged to differ. She stated, "Men need to understand that there are women who are only interested in developing relationships that can lead to commitment and hopefully marriage. I am one of those women. I do want to get to know the man first because I'm looking first for a friend. I'm looking for a man that I can communicate with, one who has self-respect and respects me and other women, a man who is honest, trustworthy, supportive, thoughtful, and caring. I believe that relationships should be based on two people working together to achieve the same goals. To me, the ultimate goals are to like and love each other. You need to enjoy each other's company and enjoy talking to each other. You need to have similar values and interests. That's what a relationship is about. Until I meet someone who believes what I believe, I don't see any need to have sex with a man simply because I can. I have decided to wait until I meet the type of man I'm looking for. I will just be by myself until then."

The above statements caused a male to make an interesting comment. He proclaimed, "I hate to tell you women this, but you won't find that kind of man living and breathing. That kind of man can only be found at a museum or in your fantasy land. You are dreaming, and what you said sounds good but that's about it. It is not realistic thinking. Waiting until this 'museum man' comes along before you have sex is nonsense. I don't know why you women are always talking about saving it. You can't take it with you when you die, so why save it? I guess you want your tombstone to read: Here lies a woman who preserved herself for sex in Heaven with a God-sent, anointed man. Good luck on your Heavenly orgasms."

The group, men and women alike, laughed uncontrollably after hearing the aforementioned comments. Once the laughter subsided and a calmer discussion ensued, it became crystal clear that the group was divided across gender lines. The forum ended with the men holding tenaciously to their position and the women not bulging an inch off of theirs. These extreme points of view may help to explain, in part, some of the problems men and women have in relationships. From all accounts, the problems will not go away anytime soon.

At a different focus group session, a discussion started about the need for men to have multiple partners and how this need helps to explain the sexual differences between males and females. In the promotion of this line of thought, a male stated, "I watch a lot of movies about animals on the Discovery Channel, and I have concluded that when it comes to sex, females need to understand that men are like other males in the animal kingdom. We are animalistic. We are programmed to have multiple partners. We are programmed to spread our seeds as far and as wide as possible. Monogamy for males is an exception, not the rule. Those males who are monogamous suppress their biological sexual proclivity to have sex with many females. Their suppression is caused by some ethical, religious, or moral belief that goes against what nature and the lower heart [their penis] dictates. They are acting out of some moral sense of righteousness." A female immediately replied, "That's just an excuse to justify your whorish ways and your lack of self-control." The male followed with, "No, that is the truth!" At this point, another female lamented, "Well, how do you explain the sexual behavior of females?" The male responded, "Females are programmed from a maternal and nurturing perspective. They are programmed to sustain the species. They are programmed to perpetuate the population. Their perspective is totally practical. It is even essential to the survival of the species." The females began to talk at the same time. They went into a verbal tirade, expressing opposition to this point of view in vociferous and angry tones. When the verbal dust settled, one female asked the male who made the comments if he had been living on Pluto. His response was, "You women can't handle the truth. That's why you don't do any better than you do in relationships." If ever a discussion had males pitted at one end of the spectrum and women at the other, this was it.

This dialogue speaks only to a portion of the description of the Gas and Go Player. There is still much more to come in the analysis of who he is.

Don't Call Me; I'll Call You

The Gas and Go Player swears by, believes in, and acts out of a mentality that demonstrates a detached, disengaged, and morally dismissive posture in male-female relationships. His goal, as one noted, is to "cop and blow." The translation of this goal is simple: Get the sex and be on your way until the next time you want it. He is the consummate escape artist. Here today, gone today. In addition, he does not promise to return to the woman. In support of this belief, one man said that this type male can dismiss a woman "*before quick gets ready.*" Now that's quick.

The behavior of these men can be compared to the behavior of patrons at neighborhood stores known as In and Out. People who live in the area go to these stores knowing exactly what they want. To them, the stores are convenient, easily accessible, and stock items that can be used to satisfy their hunger, quench their thirst, and take care of some other desires that have nothing to do with food or drink. Once they purchase these items, they don't loiter or linger. They get what they came to get and then they leave. Such is the behavior of the Gas and Go Player when he goes to his sex partner's house to have his sexual needs and wants met. Once they are met, he leaves. He has no remorse about or trepidation for his action. By his definition of the situation, he has done no wrong. He only did what he was allowed to do with a woman who was a willing participant. She was not a coerced victim. He was merely the recipient of her sexual generosity. To that end, he sees no reason to feel guilty about his behavior.

To reinforce his guiltlessness, one male stated that as he departs his sex partner's dwelling, he tells her with a smile on his face, "Don't call me. I'll call you. If she's my standby p—y, I really don't want her bugging me and 'blowing up' my cell phone." He was asked, "Aren't you concerned about her 'blowing up' your land phone?" He replied, "No, because I didn't give her my home number." He was also asked, "Why not?" His response was, "When I am taking care of business at my house with another woman, I don't want to be disturbed. Ain't no woman gonna have my home number. They can have my cell number. Some don't need that number either 'cause they don't know how to act. For example, I was involved with this one woman and she would call me five and six times a day while I was at work. I had to let her go and change my cell number. Some of these women get too possessive. They act like they haven't ever had good sex before I gave it to them. It's pitiful the way they act." Since virtually all elements in society have a rank order, it appears, at least from this male's point of view, that the home telephone number has a higher ranking than the cell number. This implies that men rank women as deserving no phone number, deserving cell number only, and rarely deserving of the land number, for those who have a land line, or all numbers. Women, what number or numbers do you have?

Sexually Moving and Grooving

The Gas and Go Player avoids a stationary, settled life with women with whom he is sexually involved. His casual attitude demonstrates a type of man who is on the prowl. He seeks out high-octane women who are low maintenance. High-octane by his definition means that the women are so sexually driven, they are willing to have sex with him whenever he wants it, no strings attached. They are low maintenance because they only require him to have good sex with them that culminates in an orgasm. They don't need romance from him or a social life with him. They don't require that he takes them out on a date or helps them with home maintenance chores. The sexual gratification and satisfaction are sufficient for them to sustain a "get the sex and go" relationship. The philandering behavior of these males and their sexually willing partners allows them to enjoy many sexual encounters with different women. During a Life Talk session in a class on male-female relationships, a female posed the question, "Why do some men only want a woman for sex?" A male responded, "That's like asking why a dog wags his tail." The female then said, "So why does a dog wag his tail?" The male responded, "Because he can, that's why." The men who seek out "for sex only" women claim to find them without any difficulty at all. In an effortless motion of comfort, these men sexually move and groove, in and out, of their sexual connections. The portrait of the Gas and Go Player has been framed. The three faces of these males will now be uncovered.

Hit-and-Run

In the vehicular vernacular, a hit-and-run is described as a driver who hits a pedestrian with his vehicle and leaves the scene of the crime. His behavior indicates that he is without culpability in spite of the crime he has committed. In the Gas and Go Player vernacular, hit-and-run relates to the male sexual connections with females for the sole purpose of filling his sexual libido tank. He is motivated by the sexual satisfaction of his sexual urges and impulses. He seeks out women who will fulfill this need upon request. He is not interested in getting to know who she is as a person. He is not concerned about her wants, needs, desires, hopes, and dreams as they relate to a meaningful, committed male-female relationship. As long as she satisfies his sexual needs, he has no complaints. Relationship bonding and attachment are not on his sexual agenda.

Following the sexual conquest, he makes a fast dash to her door and leaves. At best, he tells her, “See you later.” Since “later” is in a limitless, never ending time zone, it is whenever he gets back with her. After all, he came with no commitment to her and he departs with the same sentiments. He has achieved what he set out to achieve—get the sex and leave. He is now on the run to another woman’s sexual borders to perform the same sexual feat. His sexual motto toward women is clear and concise: Hit it, quit it, and forsake it.

The Predatory Prowler

The Predatory Prowler is always in search of the female sexual terrain, located approximately 9 inches below her navel and 14 inches above her knees on her anatomy. His prowling behavior allows him to roam female territories at will. His sexual roaming behavior and the women's response to it varies markedly from "roaming" as defined by cell phone companies. Unlike cell phone companies, the women do not charge him roaming fees. He is exempt from paying usage charges, a service fee, and late fees. His sexual wireless connection affords him unlimited day, night, and weekend minutes, unlimited rollover minutes, and unrestricted spontaneous contacts. Consequently, he roams, and roams, and roams, from one woman to another, free of charge, achieving orgasm, after orgasm, after orgasm. As one gas and go player stated, "A nut is a nut; I don't care who gives me a nut."

He also plays a clever game of trivial sexual pursuit. First, he convinces women that a "sexual encounter only relationship" is all they need with him. Second, he challenges them to put forth their best sexual skills in hopes of outperforming other women sexually. He encourages them to bring their sexual A-game to the sexual intercourse ball park. He goes on to assure them that the more sexual talents, abilities, and expertise they exhibit, the greater their chances are of winning the sexual game. Further, he congratulates them on their superior sexual performance. And last, he lets them know that their supreme mastery of sex will guarantee that he will come back and he will give them the opportunity to impress him again in the next game of sexual trivial pursuit. By now you may be asking, does this strategy really work for him? In the words of one predatory prowler, "All you have to do is tell a woman how great she is sexually and how no other woman has ever made you feel the way she does and you can go back to her for more sex as much as you want." Does this answer your question?

The Hardhearted Houdini

Harry Houdini, the world-renowned magician and escapologist, was most famous for his disappearing acts; now you see him, now you don't. Some of his most celebrated and notable escapes were the Suspended Straitjacket, the Overboard Box Escape, and the Buried Alive. The genius of Houdini seen in his magical undertakings was so unimaginable, it defied laws of gravity. It redefined the longevity of respiratory functions and it made water appear to have built-in inhalers. It must be remembered that he conquered these magical escapes with things, not people.

Chapter 4: The Gas and Go Player

In comparison to Harry Houdini, the Hardhearted Houdini types practice disappearing acts that use women as the key part of their act. These males do not care if women try to use jails, handcuffs, ropes, straitjackets, locked milk cartons, or nailed packing crates as methods to trap them and keep them in their company. The men's magical sex show is to get the sex from women and escape through the quickest exit. These sexual escapologists enjoy the adventure that comes with perfecting the art of being the greatest escape artist after they give the women the best sex they have ever known. They have no interest in what the women think of them before, during, or after the sex act. The sexual experience is all that matters to them. They have an "*UNs*" mentality about their magical escapes after the sexual conquests. Their *UNs* mentality, which speaks to how they feel about women with whom they have had sex, can best be described in 15 ways:

1. Uncompassionate
2. Unfeeling
3. Unemotional
4. Unconcerned
5. Unceremonious
6. Unabashed
7. Unattached
8. Uninterested
9. Unaffected
10. Unenthusiastic
11. Undependable
12. Unconnected
13. Unimportant
14. Unsympathetic
15. Unaccountable

The Hardhearted Houdini prides himself on denying women any form of long-term bonding with him. He is adamant about his need to be free of any sustaining, significant relationships. To drive this point home, one Hardhearted Houdini stated the following about his intentions with women and their inability to "wrap him up". "I'm not about to be tied to any woman. If she thinks she has the power to reel me in like a master fisherman reels in a prime catch of the day, she will find a piece of dead tumbleweed at the end of her fishing pole." These Gas and Go Players have a myopic view of and interest in women. To them, women serve the purpose of "booty calls" only, *no more and no less.* That's their sexual story and they are sticking to it.

Below is a survey for men to complete to determine if they are Gas and Go Players. Aren't you curious about what you will discover about yourself? Enjoy!

ARE YOU A GAS AND GO PLAYER?

Directions: Answer the following questions honestly and find out if you are a Gas and Go Player. Circle the number by the answer that best fits you.

1) I don't take my sexual partner out on dates.

1. Strongly Agree

2. Agree

3. Somewhat Agree

4. Disagree

5. Strongly Disagree

2) I don't buy my sexual partner anything, even for birthdays and Christmas.

1. Strongly Agree

2. Agree

3. Somewhat Agree

4. Disagree

5. Strongly Disagree

3) I don't talk to my sexual partner unless the conversation includes sex.

1. Strongly Agree

2. Agree

3. Somewhat Agree

4. Disagree

5. Strongly Disagree

4) I don't let my sexual partner talk about a committed relationship.

1. Strongly Agree

2. Agree

3. Somewhat Agree

4. Disagree

5. Strongly Disagree

5) I do little to no foreplay or after-play with my sexual partner.

1. Strongly Agree

2. Agree

3. Somewhat Agree

4. Disagree

5. Strongly Disagree

6) I don't want people who know me to see me with my sexual partner.

1. Strongly Agree

2. Agree

3. Somewhat Agree

4. Disagree

5. Strongly Disagree

7) I never give my sexual partner money.

1. Strongly Agree

2. Agree

3. Somewhat Agree

4. Disagree

5. Strongly Disagree

8) My sexual partner must give me sex any way I want it.

1. Strongly Agree

2. Agree

3. Somewhat Agree

4. Disagree

5. Strongly Disagree

9) My sexual partner must give me sex any time I want it.

1. Strongly Agree

2. Agree

3. Somewhat Agree

4. Disagree

5. Strongly Disagree

10) My sexual partner must give me sex anywhere I want it.

1. Strongly Agree

2. Agree

3. Somewhat Agree

4. Disagree

5. Strongly Disagree

11) My sexual partner knows that I am mainly the receiver during the sex act; I do the bare minimum.

1. Strongly Agree

2. Agree

3. Somewhat Agree

4. Disagree

5. Strongly Disagree

12) My sexual partner never gets money from me for any reason.

1. Strongly Agree

2. Agree

3. Somewhat Agree

4. Disagree

5. Strongly Disagree

13) My sexual partner knows not to ask me about my relationships with other women.

1. Strongly Agree

2. Agree

3. Somewhat Agree

4. Disagree

5. Strongly Disagree

14) My sexual partner knows that she can see me only when I am horny for her.

1. Strongly Agree

2. Agree

3. Somewhat Agree

4. Disagree

5. Strongly Disagree

15) My sexual partner knows not to mention the word "love" to me.

1. Strongly Agree
2. Agree
3. Somewhat Agree
4. Disagree
5. Strongly Disagree

16) My sexual partner knows not to ask me when she will see me again.

1. Strongly Agree
2. Agree
3. Somewhat Agree
4. Disagree
5. Strongly Disagree

17) My sexual partner has low self-esteem.

1. Strongly Agree
2. Agree
3. Somewhat Agree
4. Disagree
5. Strongly Disagree

18) My sexual partner would love to have more than a sexual relationship with me.

1. Strongly Agree
2. Agree
3. Somewhat Agree
4. Disagree
5. Strongly Disagree

19) My sexual partner is happy when I call her for some sex.

1. Strongly Agree

2. Agree

3. Somewhat Agree

4. Disagree

5. Strongly Disagree

20) My sexual partner will remain my sexual partner until I get tired of her.

1. Strongly Agree

2. Agree

3. Somewhat Agree

4. Disagree

5. Strongly Disagree

Now, it is time to add your points and determine your total points.

Rating Scale

Strongly Agree = 5 points

Agree = 4 points

Somewhat Agree = 3 points

Disagree = 2 points

Strongly Disagree = 1 point

Look at the scale below and see where you fit:

Scoring Scale

90-100 = You are definitely a Gas and Go Player.

89-80 = You are a Gas and Go Player.

79-70 = You may be a Gas and Go Player.

69-60 = You are not a Gas and Go Player.

59 and below = You are definitely not a Gas and Go Player.

Women, it is now your turn.

ARE YOU IN AN INTIMATE SEXUAL RELATIONSHIP WITH A GAS AND GO PLAYER?

Directions: Answer the following questions honestly and find out if you are in an intimate sexual relationship with a Gas and Go Player. Circle the number by the answer that best fits you.

1) My man with whom I have sex does not take me out on a date.

1. Strongly Agree

2. Agree

3. Somewhat Agree

4. Disagree

5. Strongly Disagree

2) My man doesn't buy me anything, not even a birthday or Christmas card.

1. Strongly Agree

2. Agree

3. Somewhat Agree

4. Disagree

5. Strongly Disagree

3) My man primarily talks to me about sex.

1. Strongly Agree
2. Agree
3. Somewhat Agree
4. Disagree
5. Strongly Disagree

4) My man and I never talk about a committed relationship.

1. Strongly Agree
2. Agree
3. Somewhat Agree
4. Disagree
5. Strongly Disagree

5) My man doesn't like to engage in foreplay or after-play when we have sex.

1. Strongly Agree
2. Agree
3. Somewhat Agree
4. Disagree
5. Strongly Disagree

6) My man doesn't take me out in public.

1. Strongly Agree
2. Agree
3. Somewhat Agree
4. Disagree
5. Strongly Disagree

7) My man never gives me any money.

1. Strongly Agree

2. Agree

3. Somewhat Agree

4. Disagree

5. Strongly Disagree

8) I must give my man sex any way he wants it.

1. Strongly Agree

2. Agree

3. Somewhat Agree

4. Disagree

5. Strongly Disagree

9) I must give my man sex any time he wants it.

1. Strongly Agree

2. Agree

3. Somewhat Agree

4. Disagree

5. Strongly Disagree

10) I must give my man sex anywhere he wants it.

1. Strongly Agree

2. Agree

3. Somewhat Agree

4. Disagree

5. Strongly Disagree

11) My man does the bare minimum to satisfy me when we have sex.

1. Strongly Agree

2. Agree

3. Somewhat Agree

4. Disagree

5. Strongly Disagree

12) I wish my man loved me.

1. Strongly Agree

2. Agree

3. Somewhat Agree

4. Disagree

5. Strongly Disagree

13) I can never ask my man about relationships he has with other women.

1. Strongly Agree

2. Agree

3. Somewhat Agree

4. Disagree

5. Strongly Disagree

14) I can only see my man when he is horny for me.

1. Strongly Agree

2. Agree

3. Somewhat Agree

4. Disagree

5. Strongly Disagree

15) My man doesn't want me to mention the word "love" to him.

1. Strongly Agree

2. Agree

3. Somewhat Agree

4. Disagree

5. Strongly Disagree

16) My man doesn't want me to ask him if I will see him again.

1. Strongly Agree

2. Agree

3. Somewhat Agree

4. Disagree

5. Strongly Disagree

17) My man knows that I have low self-esteem.

1. Strongly Agree

2. Agree

3. Somewhat Agree

4. Disagree

5. Strongly Disagree

18) My man knows that I would love to have more than a sexual relationship with him.

1. Strongly Agree

2. Agree

3. Somewhat Agree

4. Disagree

5. Strongly Disagree

19) I am always happy to hear from my man.

1. Strongly Agree

2. Agree

3. Somewhat Agree

4. Disagree

5. Strongly Disagree

20) I will be with my man as long as he lets me.

1. Strongly Agree

2. Agree

3. Somewhat Agree

4. Disagree

5. Strongly Disagree

Women, it is rating and scoring time.

Rating Scale

Strongly Agree = 5 points

Agree = 4 points

Somewhat Agree = 3 points

Disagree = 2 points

Strongly Disagree = 1 point

Scoring Scale

90-100 = You are definitely in a relationship with a Gas and Go Player.

89-80 = You are in a relationship with a Gas and Go Player.

79-70 = You may be in a relationship with a Gas and Go Player.

69-60 = You are not in a relationship with a Gas and Go Player.

59 and below = You are definitely not in a relationship with a Gas and Go Player.

Chapter 5

The As-Is Player

My women are women who never close
Their legs, hearts and arms
I come to them ragged, rough and raw
And they still can't resist my charm

They act like I'm the voodoo man
'Cause I put them under my spell
If I dig a hole
They drop their buckets
In the pits of my "sex you up" well

They don't care that I have no class
Job, car, house or money
They put up with anything
Just to say "I have a man"
When I really don't qualify
To be their domesticated donkey

They present me no hassles
They make no demands
Yet they jump to my every beck and call
They know I'm not worth
The salt in my bread
And they cheer me on anyway
'Cause I show out in the bed

They know I don't want them,
Like or love them
And ain't about to fulfill their needs
But they treat me like I'm their crack rock
And they are addicted to my seed

As-Is Shoppers

Have you ever seen houses sold as-is? Housing and Urban Development (HUD) is well-known for its advertisement of as-is houses. These structures are usually boarded up, with key parts in need of replacement and renovation, such as the roof, bathroom fixtures, windows, floors, kitchen counters, sinks, appliances, and painting of outside trimmings. To lure buyers, these houses are sold at bargain-basement prices. Given the depressed housing market in certain regions, some of these houses are sold for as little as $100. Those who purchase these houses understand the tremendous amount of work required to transform them into comfortable living dwellings. They commit their time, energy, effort, and money to these tasks. Some buyers undertake this endeavor so frequently that they could be referred to as "serial as-is buyers".

Automobiles are another big ticket item that can be purchased as-is. Private owners, used car businesses, dealerships, and public auctions are involved in this practice. A large number of these vehicles need new engines, transmissions, brakes, tires, and a paint job. In extreme cases, people have had to tow these as-is cars off the lot because they literally could not start. A question one may ask is: Who wants a car in such bad shape? Persons who have the auto mechanic's skills to repair them, those who have the money to pay someone to repair them, those who are involved in the restoration of vintage cars, and those who can only afford cars in these conditions are the most likely buyers.

The search for as-is material goods is a common practice among people from different walks of life for a variety of reasons. As a hobby, wealthy and well-to-do persons may enjoy tinkering with old items to restore them to a state of the art, one-of-a-kind enterprise. Less economically stable persons may acquire such commodities out of necessity, and others may have unique personal reasons that are only understood by them. As noted, the examples above are about material goods. One would think that the criteria used to select "things" differ markedly from those applied to the selection of a mate in an intimate sexual relationship. After all, you can't "fix up" a person to suit your needs, wants, desires, likes, and love treats. The treatment of a person should differ from that given to a house or a car. Houses and cars don't have brains, and they can't resist change. They primarily exist at the will of those who choose to alter their state. Let's not forget the difference material goods and human beings make. Although it is true that human beings think, act, react, and respond to others and to the environment in which they reside, it is also true that they cannot be molded and shaped by the hands of others unless they make the decision to undergo the conversion.

Chapter 5: The As-Is Player

Given these obvious revelations, the question becomes: Are there women who seek out or agree to engage in intimate sexual relationships with men who fit this As-Is category? More specifically, are there women who accept, embrace, and pursue relationships with men whose As-Is status is void of nonsexual assets that are usually required in a potentially meaningful, committed male-female intimate relationship? The bare minimum of these nonsexual assets, more often than not, include employment, a reasonable level of formal education, a place of his own, a car to drive, and at least enough ambition to acquire basic necessities of life and some niceties and amenities. The answer is *yes,* there are.

An affirmative response to the above query begs these questions: What motivates some women to accept men simply because they are breathing and have blood running through their veins? What causes some women to connect with men who have a history of chronic unemployment? What provokes some women to engage in intimate sexual relationships with men who openly and candidly expose characteristics about themselves that are seen as undesirable and uninviting by most females and the general standard used to determine marital eligibility? Is it possible that these women's vision of prospective mates is blurred, distorted, or a manifestation of an optical disorder or an optical illusion? Could they practice the art of creative visualization and use the power of positive thinking to remove the clouds from their reality of the males with whom they are involved? These questions are raised because the As-Is men do not attempt to hide virtually any aspect of themselves. In fact, they brag about how truthful they are about who they are, what they don't have, what they are not motivated to achieve, and what they are not interested in doing. From their point of view, their level of self-confidence in their ability to get any woman they want affords them the right to brag. In their own words and based on their experiences, these men will expose their trade secrets to women who accept them as-is.

The Eyes Have It

Women, when it comes to mate selection, what is your visual perception? Women's visual perception, like men's, is determined by their ability to define, interpret, and give meaning to their surroundings and the information they encounter when visible light reaches the eye. The results of the perception are known as eyesight or vision. Therefore, how women perceive men's assets and liabilities, strengths, shortcomings and weaknesses, gains and losses, and the overall appraisal or devaluation of who they are really demonstrates how women see them, why they have their sights set on certain types of men, and why their vision of these men can become *the phantom of their minds.*

Without getting too technical, when it comes to eyesight, everyone has physiological components that are collectively referred to as the visual system. The history of the study of our visual system has included both natural and social sciences in such areas as neuropsychology, cognitive science, neurophysiology, and molecular biology. What we see and how we see are of real importance to the sciences. For the purpose of this chapter, the vision of women who select As-Is men will be illustrated in a science coined here as "optic-sociology" in mate selection. It is defined as the study of the eyesight and vision of perceptions, meanings, interpretations, and definitions attached to one's learned behavior, the behavior of others, and the nature and quality of the social interaction experienced with others in intimate sexual relationships. Based on this, mate selection by women who choose these As-Is men is not determined by 20/20 vision or any vision impairment caused by or the result of some physiological factors. They are the result of social, cultural, and environmental factors that frame how people see themselves, how they behave, what they believe they deserve and do not deserve from others, how they see others, and how they see their sexual relationships.

Therefore, the vision discussed here focuses on human expectations, preferences, and the social factors that accompany them and cause some women to select men with characteristics that most women define as undesirable, unattractive, and socially unacceptable. What is the self-esteem of women who choose As-Is men? Do they think highly of themselves or do they think lowly of themselves, or some degree in between? I once counseled a woman who I defined as having the lowest self-esteem that I had ever seen in my public or private life in the mate selection category. She had attempted suicide three times. She had a history of dating drug addicts, alcoholics, criminals, ex-drug addicts, and reforming alcoholics. When I asked her if she had noticed a pattern in her mate selection, she said that she had and added, "I don't think I deserve men unless they are drug addicts, alcoholics, and men like that. I don't think I'm good enough for men who have something going for them." The last time I know of that she tried to commit suicide, she jumped from a bridge over an expressway during rush hour traffic. She did not lose consciousness, although all of her ribs were broken, her legs were broken, and she had a concussion, among other injuries. When I saw her in the hospital, her first sentence after speaking to me was, "Dr. Lewis, I know I'm a loser; I can't even kill myself right." This female's perception of herself and its affect on her mate selection choices suggest that the more lowly women think of themselves, the more likely they are to get involved with a male who has undesirable mate selection characteristics. The more highly a female thinks of herself, the more likely she is to get involved with men of desirable mate selection qualities. Other factors such as length of time a female has been without a mate, wavering on her standards, lowering her standards because she has not met a man who fits her standards, thinking she has to have sexual experiences with a man all the time, and thinking that she has to have a man are some of the intervening variables that can influence a woman's mate selection choices and criteria by which she defines "a good man".

Below is an exposé of As-Is men who were researched during the completion of this book. From an optic-sociological point of view, the remaining part of this chapter will explore the question: Do women who choose these men have an eye disorder caused by their definition of themselves, their fear of being alone, their need to feel needed, or their belief that an As-Is man will give them power and control over him?

Three-R Roy

When the phrase "the Three Rs" is used, it almost always refers to basic education at the elementary school level. It stands for reading, writing, and arithmetic. The Rs in each of these represent three basic educational skills. Do not confuse these three Rs with Three-R Roy. The latter is not related to the former in any shape, form, or fashion. Below is an example of a Three-R Roy. Do you know anyone who resembles him, or a woman who makes it possible for him to be who he is?

In the early 2000s, a 34-year-old female came to my office for a therapy session. She stated that she had a problem with the male in her life. She admitted that she met him as he was walking down the street. She also stated that he looked unkempt. His clothes were tattered and dingy. He acted unrefined and unpolished. She allows that he appeared to be a "diamond in the rough". "He stopped me to tell me how good I looked and asked me if I had a boyfriend. I thanked him for the compliment and told him that I was not involved with anyone at that time. I had ended a three-year relationship four months prior to this meeting. He asked for my telephone number and I gave it to him. He didn't offer to give me his number and I didn't ask for it. A week later, he called me." He stated that he wanted to see her and subsequently asked if she would pick him up at his favorite watering hole. She agreed and drove him to her house. She had prepared dinner for two. They dined by candlelight, drank wine, and he talked about how good he could make her feel if she would allow him to make love to her. She admitted that before the night was over, he was in her bed and they were having sex. She let him spend the night, then another night and another night. In less than two weeks, she let him move in. In this same therapy session, she revealed that this 41-year-old man did not have a job. The explanation he gave her was that he had been laid off for seven years. He said that he was waiting to be called back to work because he worked for an automotive company and the other jobs that would hire him didn't pay what he was accustomed to earning. He told her that before he was laid off, he had a house, but the layoff caused him to lose everything. When she asked him about his telephone number, he told her that he didn't have a phone at his mother's house, he didn't have a cell phone, and he couldn't give out his mother's telephone number.

She also discovered that he didn't read very well. She noted that he gave her a card for her birthday but the card had "Happy Anniversary" on the front of it. To give him the benefit of the doubt, she decided to ask him to drive her car to the store to purchase a jar of Miracle Whip. He returned with a jar of tartar sauce. She decided to ask him about his education. He told her that he dropped out of high school in the 10th grade because he was two grades behind and the teachers did not like him.

After she revealed all this information, I posed this question. "So what is your chief complaint with him?" Brace yourself for her response. In her own words, this woman with an associate of arts degree stated that her chief complaint was, "He is not attentive enough and he doesn't spend enough time with me at home." Her number one complaint had nothing to do with him being a poor reader who didn't have car, a place of his own, or a phone. It just may be true that one woman's caviar is another woman's sardines. Now, if you think you have heard it all, think again. This same woman, by her own admission, gives him money, buys his clothes, pays for his haircuts, manicures, and pedicures—yes, manicures and pedicures—and prepares his meals every day, even though she works and he doesn't.

In an effort to persuade her mate to spend more time with her, which was her major complaint, she convinced him to come to a therapy session. Of course she paid for it. Mr. Three-R Roy walked in the office with confidence and an "I am" attitude. He was well dressed and well groomed, with well-manicured nails. He quickly let it be known that he was only there to satisfy her and stop her from nagging him about coming. "She been bugging me about coming here, so I'm here." I asked him what he thought he brought to the relationship and he responded, "Everything! I make her feel good. I make her hair stand up on her head. I make her laugh. What more would any woman want?" When I asked him about finding a job and helping her with the bills, he responded, "I told her about me when we met. I didn't hide nothing. I told her I'm waiting on *them* to call me back to work. It ain't my fault they laid me off." I went on to ask him if he had any plans to go back to school and get a GED and maybe go to college to increase his chances of employment. He did not hesitate to say, "I'm not going back to school. I didn't like it when I was there. I'm too old for that stuff now. I got her without going back to school and if she wants to leave me, I can get another woman even better than her with more than she got." Without reservation, he stated that all he needed to mesmerize women was his sexual prowess, his charm, and his "gift for gab". From his point of view, in spite of his deficiencies, the women will open their arms, hearts, and legs to fulfill his wants. Ragged, rough, and raw may be more befitting for his "3 Rs". He apparently likes how he sees himself and she must like what she sees in him and what she sees that is not in him.

Pulse Rate Peter

After being asked what type of man she wants, one woman said, "One with a pulse rate. As long as he has a pulse rate, he's fair game." This type of thinking can be referred to as the Pulse Rate Mentality. After the woman made her comment, the other women in the class thought she was saying it to get a laugh. She did get a laugh, but when everyone settled down, she let them know that she was serious. "He just has to be a man. I can take it from there." How many women do you think share these sentiments about getting a man? It is impossible to determine how many women think like this because some may never admit it publicly. Therefore, I went to the men to see if any of them had played the role of Pulse Rate Peter. I set up a special class day labeled For Men Only. The men in the class were asked to invite other men who may be interested in this discussion. Thirty-three men came to the special class. They were all eager to give their definition of their "tales of conquest" with women they defined as weak. One male said, "I don't know if I am Pulse Rate Peter, but I can tell you that I have been involved with several women whose only requirement of me was to show up. They did everything else. They didn't ask me if I had a lady friend, if I were married, or if I were living with someone. It was like they didn't care what else I did as long as I spent time with them and screwed them. That was fine with me."

Another male talked about feeling like a stud because the women seemed to only want the sex. "If that's all they wanted, I could handle that." Still another man talked about his bedroom relationships. He gave it that name because he stated that he only spent time in women's bedrooms. He described one case as follows: "She would lead me directly to her bedroom and I would follow her. Afterward, I would do what the Gap Band says in one of their songs, 'put the pedal to the metal and burn rubber.' That means that I would satisfy her sexually beyond her wildest imagination. Basically, that's all you have to do. Just make them have an orgasm and you can come back as much as you want for as long as you want, and that's the truth." Still another man admitted that you have "a lot of women who are desperate. They are lonely, alone, and don't have nobody to love them. All I do is help them out. I take them out of their misery." The male who received the most applause and laughter, simultaneously, was the one who reported, "I am not just Pulse Rate Peter. I'm Pulse Rate Peter with a peter (penis). The women don't want me without my penis. Therefore, pulse rate is not enough. It has to come with the peter." His statement makes it plain, in the event it needed to be made plainer.

Jailhouse Jim

Did you know that some convicted felons are being pursued by or accommodated by women who are without a criminal record and who are gainfully employed? It's true. How do these individuals get together? Some incarcerated men join Incarcerated Personal Ads for Singles, Pen Pals for Incarcerated Men, or a similar organization that is accessible on the Internet. There are females who knew some of these males before they were incarcerated but didn't have an intimate relationship with them. Others knew them and did have an intimate relationship with them. Others have relatives serving time with the inmate and are referred to the inmate by the relative. Still others may go and visit their brother, father, nephew, or grandfather, and someone sees them and inquires about them to their relative. Since inmates have access to the television, some inmates will see a female on television and initiate correspondence with her based on the information provided on television or the information acquired from his search about her on the Internet.

Since I speak at prisons on transformation, positive mentoring, and changing a street definition of masculinity to a respectful and honorable definition of masculinity, I was allowed to interview some inmates. After asking them about relationships they have with females that could result in intimacy, some of them discussed these relationships and supplied information that gave me the opportunity to contact a few of the females. The Jailhouse Jims made interesting comments about women who found them appealing. Some of these comments were, "A whole lot of women have that fantasy 'thang'—that romantic 'thang' about relationships and life. So it's easy to fulfill their fantasies when you're locked up as opposed to being out, because being out means that the real deal is exposed and the real deal is not what you tell them on the phone and what you write in letters. Some of us compare letters to see who has the strongest rap. Some can't write too well so someone else writes the letters for them. We all know that it doesn't take a lot to satisfy these women in person and it takes much less when you're in the joint. We figure the women are lonely and we have plenty time on our hands so we might as well make them feel like somebody wants them. That's what we do and we have fun doing it. It breaks the monotony that comes with doing time."

When I asked the females why they were interested in developing a relationship with incarcerated men in hopes of becoming intimately and sexually involved with them after their release, their responses were, "I can talk to them and write to them. I look forward to their letters. I don't have to worry about another woman or other women dealing with him 'cause he's locked up. I'm lonely and it gives me someone to talk to. The things he says to me on the phone and in his letters make me feel special. He lifts my spirit. To me, the only difference in the men out here and those locked up is freedom. Other than that, they are all basically the same. They all try to run game on you, so it really doesn't matter whether he's locked up or not. When he gets out, I know that I will be his woman and he will be my man." After hearing these comments, one can gain a better understanding of why the As-Is Player is alive and well, and flourishing.

Homeless Hank

Homeless men on the streets and those who spend some of their time in shelters are not off-limits to some women. Yes, it is true that some women have taken men home with them who were in a shelter. There are claims that still others have driven to the corner where men are holding up signs that read, "will work for food," or something similar, and taken them home. A woman who was employed at a shelter began to befriend one of the men in the shelter. By her own admission, as time went on and their conversations increased, she found herself becoming attached to him and fond of him. She stated, "I saw him as a man who was down on his luck. He appeared to be a good person." This woman knew that it was against the shelter's policy for an employee to develop an intimate sexual relationship with men who were housed at the shelter. In spite of this awareness, this female began a relationship with one of the men. It wasn't long before it was discovered by her supervisor. She lost her job and the right to get a decent letter of recommendation from the shelter. She went on to admit that she was in love with this man and she couldn't help what she did. Unfortunately, this story had an ending that was worse than losing her job. She allowed him to move in her house, even though he was a former drug addict. About six months after he moved in, different items in her home disappeared. Her jewelry, laptop computer, and money were the major items he took. She was forced to put him out. Afterward, he broke into her home and physically assaulted her. He was arrested and convicted of felonious assault and home invasion. Homeless Hank was not homeless anymore. He was now a guest of the State for at least three years. More than a year after the incident, she still had not found employment and was on the verge of losing virtually all of her possessions for which she had worked.

20/20 Vision or Vision Disorders: The Eyesight of Women Who Love As-Is Players

If an ophthalmologist were asked if the eyesight of women who select As-Is Players is based on physiological factors, the answer would be an unequivocal no. However, from an "optic-sociological" point of view, women who select Three-R Roy, Pulse Rate Peter, Jailhouse Jim, or Homeless Hank may be viewed as suffering from some visual illusion, optical illusion, or some form of a social eyesight disorder. This sociologically visual illusion gives them a false or deceptive sense of visual impression. In other words, they mislead themselves in their choice of mates and the expectations that accompany them. They may also play mind games with themselves. In this context, these games are known as optical illusions. When this happens, these women visually perceive images that differ from an objective reality. They will create their own reality to suit their needs or wants at a particular time with a particular male. Sociologically speaking, their vision in mate selection and social interaction may be blurred, distorted, or cloudy, based on society's normative definition of the situation. But by these women's definition of their situation, they do not suffer sociologically from nearsightedness or farsightedness. They do not have a sty on their eye or a pink eye. They do not have cataracts or glaucoma. Their vision of choosing a mate from their point of view is *just fine, thank you.*

Men, you can complete the survey below and determine if you are one of the men these females select as a mate. Enjoy!

ARE YOU AN AS-IS PLAYER?

Directions: Answer the following questions honestly and find out if you are an As-Is Player.

Chapter 5: The As-Is Player

1) My women never try to change me.

1. Strongly Agree
2. Agree
3. Somewhat Agree
4. Disagree
5. Strongly Disagree

2) My women can't resist my charm.

1. Strongly Agree
2. Agree
3. Somewhat Agree
4. Disagree
5. Strongly Disagree

3) My women don't hassle me about anything.

1. Strongly Agree
2. Agree
3. Somewhat Agree
4. Disagree
5. Strongly Disagree

4) My women don't make demands on me.

1. Strongly Agree
2. Agree
3. Somewhat Agree
4. Disagree
5. Strongly Disagree

5) My women jump to my every beck and call.

1. Strongly Agree
2. Agree

3. Somewhat Agree

4. Disagree

5. Strongly Disagree

6) My women know that I'm not concerned about fulfilling their needs.

1. Strongly Agree

2. Agree

3. Somewhat Agree

4. Disagree

5. Strongly Disagree

7) My women are not bothered by me being unable to take care of myself.

1. Strongly Agree

2. Agree

3. Somewhat Agree

4. Disagree

5. Strongly Disagree

8) My women don't care if I don't take care of them.

1. Strongly Agree

2. Agree

3. Somewhat Agree

4. Disagree

5. Strongly Disagree

9) My women love the way I have sex with them.

1. Strongly Agree

2. Agree

3. Somewhat Agree

4. Disagree

5. Strongly Disagree

10) My women will know that I don't love them.

1. Strongly Agree

2. Agree

3. Somewhat Agree

4. Disagree

5. Strongly Disagree

11) My women act like I hypnotized them.

1. Strongly Agree

2. Agree

3. Somewhat Agree

4. Disagree

5. Strongly Disagree

12) My women always have their arms open for me.

1. Strongly Agree

2. Agree

3. Somewhat Agree

4. Disagree

5. Strongly Disagree

13) My women always have their hearts open for me.

1. Strongly Agree

2. Agree

3. Somewhat Agree

4. Disagree

5. Strongly Disagree

14) I can see my women any time I get ready.
1. Strongly Agree

2. Agree

3. Somewhat Agree

4. Disagree

5. Strongly Disagree

15) My women don't care that I don't have a car.
1. Strongly Agree

2. Agree

3. Somewhat Agree

4. Disagree

5. Strongly Disagree

16) My women don't care that I don't have a job.
1. Strongly Agree

2. Agree

3. Somewhat Agree

4. Disagree

5. Strongly Disagree

17) My women don't care that I don't have the class that they want in a man.
1. Strongly Agree

2. Agree

3. Somewhat Agree

4. Disagree

5. Strongly Disagree

18) My women know that I basically don't like them.
1. Strongly Agree

2. Agree

3. Somewhat Agree

4. Disagree

5. Strongly Disagree

19) My women give me sex whenever I come around to get it.

1. Strongly Agree

2. Agree

3. Somewhat Agree

4. Disagree

5. Strongly Disagree

20) My women act like they are addicted to me.

1. Strongly Agree

2. Agree

3. Somewhat Agree

4. Disagree

5. Strongly Disagree

Below are the rating and scoring scales for you to determine if you are an As-Is Player.

Rating Scale

Strongly Agree = 5 points

Agree = 4 points

Somewhat Agree = 3 points

Disagree = 2 points

Strongly Disagree = 1 point

Scoring Scale

90-100 = I am definitely an As-Is Player.

89-80 = I am an As-Is Player.

79-70 = I may be an As-Is Player.

69-60 = I am not an As-Is Player.

59 and below = I am definitely not an As-Is Player.

Did you anticipate these results? Did your score surprise you? Do you plan to change any aspect of your behavior in male-female relationships? The decisions, as you know, rest with you.

Women, below is the survey for you to determine the extent to which you are with an As-Is Player, or if you have had a relationship with one in the past.

ARE YOU IN AN INTIMATE SEXUAL RELATIONSHIP WITH AN AS-IS PLAYER?

Directions: Answer the following questions honestly and find out if you are in an intimate sexual relationship with an As-Is Player. Circle the number by the answer that best fits you.

1) I accept my man As-Is.

1. Strongly Agree

2. Agree

3. Somewhat Agree

4. Disagree

5. Strongly Disagree

2) I cannot resist my man's charm.

1. Strongly Agree

2. Agree

3. Somewhat Agree

4. Disagree

5. Strongly Disagree

3) I don't hassle my man about anything.

1. Strongly Agree
2. Agree
3. Somewhat Agree
4. Disagree
5. Strongly Disagree

4) I don't make any demands on my man.

1. Strongly Agree
2. Agree
3. Somewhat Agree
4. Disagree
5. Strongly Disagree

5) I will jump to my man's every call.

1. Strongly Agree
2. Agree
3. Somewhat Agree
4. Disagree
5. Strongly Disagree

6) I know that my man is not concerned about fulfilling my needs.

1. Strongly Agree
2. Agree
3. Somewhat Agree
4. Disagree
5. Strongly Disagree

7) It does not bother me that my man is unable to take care of himself.

1. Strongly Agree
2. Agree

3. Somewhat Agree

4. Disagree

5. Strongly Disagree

8) It does not bother me that my man can't take care of me.

1. Strongly Agree

2. Agree

3. Somewhat Agree

4. Disagree

5. Strongly Disagree

9) I love the way my man has sex with me.

1. Strongly Agree

2. Agree

3. Somewhat Agree

4. Disagree

5. Strongly Disagree

10) The truth is, I know my man doesn't love me.

1. Strongly Agree

2. Agree

3. Somewhat Agree

4. Disagree

5. Strongly Disagree

11) I act like my man has hypnotized me.

1. Strongly Agree

2. Agree

3. Somewhat Agree

4. Disagree

5. Strongly Disagree

12) My arms are always open for my man.
1. Strongly Agree

2. Agree

3. Somewhat Agree

4. Disagree

5. Strongly Disagree

13) My heart is always open for my man.
1. Strongly Agree

2. Agree

3. Somewhat Agree

4. Disagree

5. Strongly Disagree

14) My man can see me any time he gets ready.
1. Strongly Agree

2. Agree

3. Somewhat Agree

4. Disagree

5. Strongly Disagree

15) It does not bother me that my man doesn't have a car.
1. Strongly Agree

2. Agree

3. Somewhat Agree

4. Disagree

5. Strongly Disagree

16) It does not bother me that my man has no job.
1. Strongly Agree

2. Agree

3. Somewhat Agree

4. Disagree

5. Strongly Disagree

17) It does not bother me that my man doesn't have the class I want in a man.

1. Strongly Agree

2. Agree

3. Somewhat Agree

4. Disagree

5. Strongly Disagree

18) I believe that basically my man does not like me.

1. Strongly Agree

2. Agree

3. Somewhat Agree

4. Disagree

5. Strongly Disagree

19) I give my man sex whenever we get together.

1. Strongly Agree

2. Agree

3. Somewhat Agree

4. Disagree

5. Strongly Disagree

20) I act like I am addicted to my man.

1. Strongly Agree

2. Agree

3. Somewhat Agree

4. Disagree

5. Strongly Disagree

Chapter 5: The As-Is Player

Below are the rating and scoring scales for women to determine if they are in a relationship with an As-Is Player. Rate and score yourself.

Rating Scale

Strongly Agree = 5 points

Agree = 4 points

Somewhat Agree = 3 points

Disagree = 2 points

Strongly Disagree = 1 point

Scoring Scale

90-100 = You definitely are in a relationship with an As-Is Player.

89-80 = You are in a relationship with an As-Is Player.

79-70 = You are somewhat in a relationship with an As-Is Player.

69-60 = You are not in a relationship with an As-Is Player.

59 and below = You are definitely not in a relationship with an As-Is Player.

Did your score surprise you? Do you plan to change any aspect of your behavior in male-female relationships? The decision is yours to make.

Part II

The Betrayer Players

Betrayer Players are the perpetrators of one of the worst relationship frauds committed against womankind. These players are dangerous and masterful deceivers. Their behavior can be defined as an assault with intent to commit great emotional, psychological, and sexual harm to women. They will stab women in the heart with a machete and cut a deep hole into their self-worth and self-esteem, and pierce and puncture their belief in their intuitive and evaluative qualities used to assess men and their motives in male-female relationships. They will shoot and kill women mentally with a gun loaded with manipulative, deceitful, and conniving bullets. Under virtually no circumstances will they reveal who they really are to the women with whom they are involved. These males' behavior is rooted in and operate out of lies that tie together and collectively manifest themselves in deceit. This emotional trauma can leave a psychological scar on women that will last a lifetime.

The three categories they represent are The Silent Deceiver Player, The Philophobic Player, and The Down Low Player. Women who fall victim to these players during the first stage of the development of a relationship are not responsible for their inability to determine who they are. These men are so crafty and well-bred for the deceitful roles they play, the most skilled and educated psychiatrist, psychologist, social worker, and sociologist may find themselves clueless regarding the true motives for these men's behavior. As you read the descriptions of some of them in the next three chapters, ask yourself: Would I know that they were not who they claimed to be? Don't blame yourself if you would not. Forgive yourself for not knowing and do what you have to do to prepare yourself to know better the next time.

Chapter 6

The Silent Deceiver Player

I cover up the person I really am
With a New Orleans Mardi Gras mask
It conceals my motives
It hides my intent
The world's best psychic readers
Are still tracking my scent

I'm the architect of deception
The designer of slickness and sham
I created the wicked game called hanky-panky
I play the role of a dipsy-doodle, crafty ram

Women know I'm cunning
And I'm a flimflammer too
I'm so irresistible
They say: "Oh, what the hell
I want you and only you"

I live a life of trickery
I wrap women up in my delicious bag of tricks
They love my assorted bamboozle candy
And they crave my betrayal cookie mix

I hoodwink women
I double-cross them
I lead them to the land of astray
They come to me
In need of some sex
I gladly oblige them
With my powerful sexual lay

My motto is: "Don't tell women my secrets"
About any part of my real self
Why should I reveal
That I'm the storm in their sea
I'm the human tornadoes and hurricanes
In the lives of the women I see

I am the stranger
The silent deceiver
With a heart that's phony and fake

My only goal
With the women I meet
Is to
Rule
Control
And
Dominate.

Who Are They?

When you meet and greet other people, what criteria do you use to determine who they are? Do you evaluate their physical appearance, voice tone, choice of words, enunciation of words, or their walk, dress, facial expressions, and eye contact? What makes you decide to exchange telephone numbers or to decline the gesture when you meet someone? If you decide to talk to the person, what is your reason for making that decision? If you continue to talk, what motivates your desire to keep the phone lines open? And finally, if you accept a date, what entices you to move the relationship to this level? The answer to these questions may reveal how easy or how difficult a Silent Deceiver may be able to mislead you, and later disappoint you.

The Silent Deceiver has one major purpose in mind: To get others to believe the falsehoods he wants them to believe. Therefore, whatever these players show you, do not believe them. They perpetrate a human fraud as a means to an end. The end is simple; they want their way in the relationship. It is very clear to them that the exposure of who they really are, in all likelihood, will not afford them the leverage to misuse and take advantage of women in intimate sexual relationships. They are so proficient at what they do that one may think that universities are awarding PhDs in a new area of study called "Deceitology," and they are the recipients of the degree. If "Deceitology" were to become a science, it probably would be defined as the study of human deceptive behavior in a group context.

Some of the major games the Silent Deceivers play and the women with whom they play them will now be discussed. Pay close attention to what these deceivers do, how they do it, and how they select victims with whom to do it.

The Secretive Game

About 10 years ago, I facilitated a male-female relationship workshop attended by 23 women and 12 men whose ages ranged from 22 to 66. Initially, the women were quite vocal in expressing their concerns about men's behavior in relationships. One woman talked about how her male companion quizzed her regarding virtually every aspect of her life. Yet, when she asked him about who he was, his

family background, goals, and values, he never gave her a direct answer. She continued by saying that most of the time, he avoided the questions by giving her what I like to call "non-response responses".
These "non-response responses" are vague statements that are virtually meaningless when it comes to clarifying an inquiry. Some examples of these statements are: "You don't need to know that." "That has nothing to do with our relationship." "That is not important." "You ask too many questions." "I'm tired of you giving me the third degree." "Can't we talk about something else?"

At this point, a male raised his hand, and said, "You women do ask too many questions. If we told you everything you wanted to know about us, we would give you a road map to our hearts, and why should we do that? All you would do is take advantage of us." The conversation then moved to the topic "Strangers in Relationships," and raised the following questions: "Why should any woman desire an intimate sexual relationship with a male who wants to maintain anonymity about who he is? Why would a woman share her 'Precious Temple' (which is her body) with someone she does not know?" The discussion escalated to a more intense level, with an almost unanimous breakdown of opinions across gender lines. The women agreed that in intimate sexual relationships, both partners need to honestly and openly tell the truth about matters related to intentions about the relationship, along with personal goals, values, beliefs, habits, strengths, and shortcomings. With the exception of three men participating in this discussion, all others subscribed to remaining voiceless about who they were.

This level of secrecy suggests much more than a fear of women getting to men's hearts. It also speaks to a need for these men to hide their real selves, fearing that women will know that they are not who they claim to be.

More recently in 2007, I counseled a young woman in her late '30s. She was dating a guy she had known for four months and they went on between 9 to 12 dates. However, he refused to tell her his real name, where he lived, and where he was employed. When they dated, he told her to call him "sweet cakes". They would meet at the location of the date. When I asked her why she continued to date someone who refused to tell her who he was, her response was, "I enjoy his company and he is an intelligent man. He knows a lot about current events. When we go to concerts and jazz sets, he knows the history of the artists and the music they play. I know he's a businessman because he talks like he's an entrepreneur. I think he's a good catch." I followed that question with, "Did it bother you that he was so secretive about his true self?" She retorted, "I think he's secretive because he has money and he wants to make sure I'm not a gold digger and that I'm not after his money."

I later posed the questions, "Why do you think he has money, and if he has, how do you know he acquired it legally? And, how do you know he has a job or a business?" She stated in a most confident tone, "I just have a feeling that he has money and that he is a businessman with a legal business." She also said that his secrecy did not affect her because she was counteracting his secretiveness by refraining from divulging more information about herself. These two examples of close-lipped men are illustrations of the modus operandi of the Silent Deceiver Player, which is, "Ask, ask, if you must—just know that my answers will always be wrapped in lust".

The Dishonest Double-Crossing Game

I was conducting stress-management workshops for production workers at one of the automotive plants in metro Detroit. There were 1,500 production workers, of whom more than 90% were men. Every production worker was required to attend at least one of these workshops that were offered every Thursday over a two-year period. Most of them attended at least two or more workshops.

Since work, family, and nonmarital intimate sexual relationships are interrelated and tend to represent a disproportionate amount of the distress in the lives of adults, the emphases were on these life aspects. When discussing male-female relationships and the importance of being honest and trustworthy if you desire a healthy, wholesome relationship, a male raised his hand and said, "Women don't want you to tell them the truth. They can't handle the truth. They want you to lie to them as long as the lies stroke their egos. So, I just lie to them and tell them what they want to hear. When you lie to them and tell them how beautiful they are and how great they are in bed, they will do anything you want them to do, when you want them to do it, and the way you want them to do it."

Other men chimed in with phrases of agreement. They talked about how lying to women about what they want to hear scores the most points. Their position was that the more devious, defrauding, and dishonest they were, the more pleased women were. "That's how we make them happy. We charm them and tell them how much we love them and adore them." Dishonesty for them had become a way of life in their intimate sexual relationships. Thus, lies and deceit toward their mates became their stress relievers.

In a therapy session, a male discussed why he had no desire to become monogamous in his sexual conquests. He claimed that he was having too much fun with several women. During the session, he mentioned how women asked the wrong questions at the most inopportune times. I asked him to give an example of what he meant. He stated that he was engaged in sex with a woman and during the act, she asked him if he loved her. His response was "yeah." He went on, "What do women expect you to say at a time like that? You would have to be a moron to say, 'No, I don't love you and I never did. This is a sex "thang" only.'"

Chapter 6: The Silent Deceiver Player

For these men, it is gratifying and satisfying to be dishonest. They would probably take the position that the means justify the rewards at the end.

A Silent Deceiver Player Defined by *His* Definition of the Situation

W. I. Thomas (1928), a sociologist, developed a theorem known as the Definition of the Situation. It says quite simply: If people define situations as real, then that definition will become their reality in its consequences. To apply this to the Silent Deceiver, it means that the Silent Deceiver Player develops his own falsehood of who he wants women to believe he is, and he intentionally creates a social reality that does not have the slightest resemblance to who he really is. He then acts out the delusions he created. In relationships, intimate sexual ones included, people tend to give themselves definitions about who they are. They form perceptions about the situations in which they find themselves. They attach a meaning to their behavior, and they interpret their behavior as well as the behavior of others. The images people construct of themselves is oftentimes rooted in this type of self-analysis.

Using these same criteria, the Silent Deceiver Player carves out his definition of himself and acts out that definition in his relationships. The categories below explain the breadth and depth of some of these multidimensional men. The characterizations presented are mainly in the first person. They illustrate a compilation of the thought process of Silent Deceivers that was exposed during therapy sessions, Life Talk sessions, and at seminars and forums.

The Masterful Manipulator

"I am bossy and controlling. I tell women what to do, how to do it and when to do it. It's my way or no way. I control the minds of my women. They think the way I want them to think. They act the way I want them to act. They dress the way I want them to dress. They talk the way I want them to talk. They move when I tell them to move. We have sex only when I want to."

As an example of a maniacal-controlling personality, a male once told me that if he had his way, his woman would not leave the house without his permission. He revealed, "To keep her at home, I would tie her to the bed. When I would allow her to leave home, I would blindfold her so she couldn't see anyone. I would handcuff her so she couldn't wave her hand to anyone. I would put chains around her ankle so she couldn't strut when she walked. And I would put a muzzle on her mouth so she couldn't talk to anyone. I would also tell her that it is in her best interest to do things my way because I have the superior mind. Moreover, superior minds think superior thoughts. I will convince her that she needs me and she can't make it without me. My goal is to get her to believe that no one loves her but me. After I get her to believe me and believe in me, she will believe that I am her 'all in all'."

This type of thinking is by far the epitome of what can be referred to as the pathology of dominance.

The Cagey Critter

"I dupe women into believing that I am trustworthy, reliable, and dependable. I do what they tell me to do. If they need to go somewhere, I become their chauffeur. If something needs repairing at their home, I become their handyman. When they are hungry, I become their chef. And when they need to discuss a personal matter with someone, I become their confidant. Furthermore, I give them plenty of good sex. I tell them that my sole purpose in life is to please them and make them happy.

"I persuade them to believe that they are the best thing that ever happened to me. I paint a picture that depicts the alleged void and emptiness that were in my life before I met them. I tell them that before I met them, I didn't think I would find someone who could make me happy. And last, I tell them that my life is sexually and intimately prosperous, and completely fulfilled because they are the center of my life.

"Keep in mind that I am the artful, cunning mixture of some of the slickest animals on the face of this earth. I know more about the behavior of animals than a zookeeper. I act as if I have 30 years of professional experience in animal psychology. I am king of the animal kingdom because I know the type of animal behavior that will give me the results I want from the women in my life. Sometimes I act like a well-trained dog. When my women say 'sit,' I sit. When they need to feel protected, I become their guard dog. On other days, I may need to play the role of a chameleon, and change colors at will. In this role, I become who they want me to be, if it gets me what I want from them and if it's something I don't object to doing. When they need me to be sexually on fire, I turn blood red. When they want me to act like I can sing like Prince, I turn into 'Purple Rain'. When they need money, within the amount I am willing to give, I turn money green. When my women need to pet and pamper me, I pretend to be in a blue mood. My lapdog, fake behavior is so convincing, the women think that they have full control over me.

"I talk about being depressed because I pretend that I want to do more for them, but I just don't have the money to do as much as I really desire to do. I tell them how I would love to buy them a mansion and a luxury car of their choice. I convince them that I don't think anything is too good for them. At other times, I play the role of a man whose intelligence elevates him to a high altitude level. I act as if I have acquired enough knowledge to solve any problem they have. In addition to my intellectual knowledge, I let them know that my common sense and mother wit are hard to match.

"At this point, they are so into me that their IQ shrinks from its normal size of 125, 160, or 200 and becomes their dress size of a 2, 4, 10, or 12. Sometimes it becomes their shoe size, such as a 5 medium,

9 wide, or 10 narrow. I can also put on my obedient hat and act as if I will do anything for them. I have perfected this role so well, they think I'm their homing pigeon. I will play the role of a delivery bird and take messages to any person and to any place.

"When I decide to act really sneaky, I turn into the slickest sly fox. I am such a wizard at this role that one would think I put the 'sly' in sly fox. I sometimes play the role of the fox that guards the hen house, while knowing that I am not the least bit interested in the hen. The hen sees me as protective, loving, caring, and dependable. Sometimes in my sly fox role, I use statements that don't make sense. For example, there was a woman who loved to hear me say that I will kill a dead stump over her. She would smile and blush every time I said it. She would brag to her girlfriends about the statement. She didn't realize that you can't kill something that's already dead. And even if you could, it was only a stump. It's just a small piece of the trunk of a felled or fallen tree."

The Shrewd Shyster

"I pay so much attention to women, they think I can read their minds. I think I can read their minds. I know what women are thinking before they express a thought. Although I know what they want, I don't always give it to them. I fulfill their needs that will benefit me and that will give me good returns on the investment of my time. I encourage them to tell me what they want. They are assured that their wish is my command.

"As an example of my skillfulness in matters of women, I must share a story that occurred on Valentine's Day. I was invited to one woman's home for a Valentine's dinner. After she set out a six-course meal, I escorted her to her bedroom to express my appreciation sexually. She was overwhelmed and completely satisfied. Upon leaving, she gave me a box of Godiva chocolates and a dozen of long-stemmed red roses. After I left her house, I called another female I was dating and told her I was coming over to bring her a Valentine's gift. The same chocolates and roses given to me by the other woman were given to this woman. She was ecstatic. She talked about how glad she was to see me. She said that since it was so late (it was around 10:00 p.m.), she thought I had forgotten about her. It shows the canny way I present gifts to women and how I present myself. The second woman would never believe that another woman gave me the Valentine's gifts I gave her. Is that shrewd or is that shrewd?"

The Crafty Conqueror

"I have an 'I must win' mentality. Not only must I win, I must win by any means necessary. At the time I am winning, I assure the women that they are winning. I use the approach Muhammad Ali used as a boxer to accomplish this feat. Ali used his patented rope-a-dope style to get his opponents to believe that he was tired. Thus, he would lean on the ropes and appear as if he had nothing left with which to fight. When his opponents thought they had won, he would leave the ropes and come out fighting. They would be shocked, amazed, and aghast. I have gone so far as to wave the white flag, symbolizing that I surrender. When this happened, the women thought that they had the upper hand and had won the relationship battle. If truth were told, they not only lost the relationship battle, they lost the relationship war.

"A situation occurred between two women I was dating. They found out that I was dealing with both of them. The one who I had really convinced that she had the upper hand told the other that her time was up. She was so confident that she was the only woman with whom I was involved, she felt that she could speak for my feelings, my heart, and my thoughts about the other woman. I didn't tell her differently because with the confidence she expressed about how I felt toward the other woman, I knew I had won with her in grand style. My style resembled the likes of Justin Verlander of the Detroit Tigers, who became the first starting pitcher in a quarter-century to be voted the American League's Most Valuable Player and also win the Cy Young Award, both in 2011. Or the style was similar to Buck Buchanan, a Grambling State University graduate who was the first African American number one draft choice in professional football by the Kansas City Chiefs. And finally, the style had the likeness of Bill Russell when he won an unprecedented eighteen NBA championships."

Remember, the Crafty Conqueror has a "must-win" mentality. He is bound and determined to win at all costs.

The Clever Counterfeiter

"I am an all-around, quick-witted imitation of who I say I am and who I act as if I am. My impersonation of whom I like to call 'the many faces of Adam to fool Eve and other women' is strategically designed and orchestrated to mislead women. I am as much of a forgery as a $4.00 bill. Yet, I will say, 'You can take that to the bank,' when I know that you cannot. I will admit that my bank vault consists of language, facial expressions, gestures, signs, and symbols that are bogus. When talking to my women, I use endearing words like 'sweetheart', 'darling', 'baby', and 'baby cakes'. The women think I really see them as special in my life, as the words suggest. It would be to their chagrin if they ever found out the truth.

"The truth is that I use those words to avoid calling them the wrong name. I try to look at them with the dreamiest 'I adore you' eyes. I wink at them. I smile when I see them so that they will think that I am Joseph Brooks, the composer of 'You Light up My Life'. I hug them every chance I get. I lightly pinch them on the cheek. I plant light kisses on their forehead and on their lips. I buy them beautiful romantic cards for special occasions and for no occasions. With all of my artificial behavioral sweeteners, I'm even surprised that women take me to be 'The Bona Fide Beau'. I guess I am so great at my game and talented in my interpersonal, lovable skills, the women find me irresistible."

The moral of this story for players is: Why show your real self when your phony self works so well?

The Sham Suitor

"I love to play many games. However, my favorite game by far is 'Let's pretend'. Let's pretend that I am pursuing her, dating her, and courting her to marry her in the very near future. I have not purchased an engagement ring. I take her to her favorite jewelry stores for her to look at rings. Remember, this game is 'Let's Pretend'. Additionally, I make statements regarding a future marriage, such as: When you become my wife, we will travel. I will spoil you. I will shower you with gifts. I will make you the center of my life. I woo her with much vim and vigor. I take her out to look at houses from which we will select our dream home, so she thinks. I purchase travel magazines so we can choose our honeymoon location. By this time, she is telling her family members, friends, and coworkers that she will marry the love of her life. She hasn't stopped to realize that I never asked her to marry me."

This game was played on one woman who came to me for counseling. She stated that her mate had told her virtually everything stated above. Two years later, he was still telling the same string of lies. He extended his conversation to include reasons why they needed to wait a little longer before they could get married. He told her that he needed more time to get out of debt, more time to earn more money, more time to wait on his next promotion, and more time to let him find out if he could trust her. She became so impatient, she purchased an engagement ring and told her relatives, friends, and coworkers that her mate had purchased it. When she was in his company, she would not wear the ring.

She extended tales about her relationship to include that they were secretly married. She even took on his last name. When those who knew her found out it was not true, she was embarrassed. Now, she needed her therapist to guide her out of this maze of embarrassment she created. "Let truth prevail," was my advice. There's a concept, coined by sociologist Max Weber in one of his writings called *uncomfortable truths.* He asserted that even when truth is uncomfortable and sometimes painful, tell the truth anyway. When I advise people on truth, I stress the fact that *truth is liberating; truth is freedom.*

She may find it distressing and uncomfortable to admit to others that she lied. However, those to whom she lied usually know she lied anyway.

The Trickery Tranquilizer

"I make October 31, Halloween, come alive in relationships. Well, sort of but not quite. I put a little twist in it. I 'treat' to solidify my 'trick'. In a very serene and methodical way, I put my plan in motion. My goal was to 'soothe my women's restless spirit' by sedating them with my drug of 250 milligrams of charm and 500 milligrams of finesse. They were so taken off their feet by my smooth and perceptive power, they couldn't keep their composure. No one would think that my intentions were not honorable, because I looked so innocent and I acted so reserved."

The calm meanness in the above case was witnessed at a home of one of my friends. My girlfriend's mother was visiting her and she invited me to have dinner with them. She informed me that her new beau would be there to dine with us. During dinner, her male friend did not say a word unless someone asked him a question. Even then, his responses were no more than one-three words. I first thought that since the women outnumbered him by three-one, he felt uncomfortable. That was not the case. He had to leave and go to work before I left. My friend's mother asked her daughter how long she had known him. Where did she meet him? Moreover, is he always that quiet? Her daughter answered, "I have known him six months. I met him at a nightclub. He is always quiet." The mother responded, "Beware of persons who say very little. You know the old saying: '*Still waters run deep*.'" Maybe, just maybe, the reason they have so little to say is because they have a lot to hide. As time went on, the mother's proverbial wisdom proved accurate. The guy later revealed his real self, characterized by moodiness, unwarranted anger, and evilness. With this behavior, he unequivocally demonstrated the "trick" in his trick or treat.

The many dimensions of the Silent Deceiver Player are not exhausted here, by any stretch of the imagination. The above mentioned typologies lay the foundation for a better understanding of who they are and the motivation attached to their behavior. To more fully understand how the Silent Deceivers define their abilities to fool women, the statements below typify how they believe they can manipulate and fool women. The phrases encapsulate the games they play and their perceptions of their successes.

I lead women astray
I pull women's legs
I take women for a ride
I engage in double-dealing with women
I pull the wool over women's eyes
I put something over on women
I outwit women
I throw women off the scent
I double-cross women
I outfox women

Chapter 6: The Silent Deceiver Player

These games of action are sometimes woven in with games characterized by inaction. For example, nonverbal behavior can translate to a powerful form of communication. Although words are not spoken, body language can speak a profound, unspoken thought. Below is more of an explanation of the downside of silence.

Silence Is Ghastly

The ghastly part of silence occurs when it is used to hide the real motives of one's behavior from the deceived person. My favorite quote by Dr. Maya Angelou is, "When people show you who they are, believe them." This powerful quote is true except for the Betrayers in general and the Silent Deceiver Player in particular. Anyone who sets out to create an image and definition of himself that does not exist, the application of the above quote is rendered null and void. Since the most educated psychiatrists, psychologists, social workers, and sociologists cannot read minds, reliance on observation, intuition, educated guesses, and the nuances of people's verbal expressions are used to principally get a sense of who they are. The use of silence as a mask to disguise one's true intentions can have unthinkable consequences. Beware a person who literally quizzes you about who you are and yet acts as if they have no past, present, or future goals to share with you.

Liars vs. Deceivers

If you can talk, you have lied. An 11-month-old baby boy's mother can tell him not to touch the stove and as soon as she is not looking at him, he will invariably touch it. When the mother asks her child, "Did you touch the stove?" The child almost always says no. In spite of the fact that legend states that George Washington never told a lie, if there were a lie to be told, and there was, you can assume that he told one, or two, or three, or more. The point is, everyone has lied and fallen short of the truth. On the other hand, not everyone has been deceitful. Deceit is a calculated, methodical, deliberate plan of action designed to convince someone that an untruth is true. It takes a series of lies threaded together to paint a deceitful falsehood. It is insidious, intentional, and manipulative. Accompanied by malice and fraud, deceivers are fully conscious of their behavior. The victims of deceit feel misused, abused, and betrayed when they discover the deceit. The treacherous behavior of deceivers can manifest in very dangerous outcomes. Injuries, assaults, mutilation, and even death have resulted from deceit. Do not assume that you are *too smart* to be fooled by skillful deceivers. Very intelligent women as well as street-smart women have fallen prey to their rhetoric.

Women's Initial Perceptions of the Silent Deceiver Player

I attended a banquet with family members and friends. We shared a table with a group unknown to us prior to the gathering. One of the women in the group dominated the conversation talking about this guy she met. She went on and on about how wonderful he was and how he was all she could ever imagine in a man in her life. She was truly singing his praises. She stated how compatible they were, how romantic he was, how protective, caring, sharing, and charming he was. To her, he was the best thing that happened to her since she received her master's degree. One of my relatives asked her, "How long have you known him?" The woman retorted, "I have known him for four months." My relative then asked her, if she didn't object, could she have her number and call her about six months later? The lady asked why. My relative stated, "I want to know if you will be saying the same things about him then."

About a year passed before I spoke to my relative again. During our conversation, I recalled the verbal exchange she had with the woman at the banquet. I asked her if she had talked to the woman. She replied in the affirmative. I asked, "Did you ask her about the guy she bragged about at the banquet?" She said, "Yes." I then asked, "What did she say about her male friend?" She said the woman sounded so sad and pitiful. She told me that during the conversation, the woman began to sob. The woman explained to her that about a month after the banquet, the man turned out to be 200 pounds of deceit in a male's body. She said the man had lied to her about virtually everything. He had claimed to have two college degrees. He had none. He said that he was earning in the six figures. He didn't make more than $30,000. He told her that his mother was living with him because she was financially incapable of caring for herself. The truth was that he was living with her. She also discovered that he had three children and that he was not paying child support. I stopped her and said, "I have heard enough."

This story is just one illustration of the crafty, devious, and fraudulent behavior of a Silent Deceiver. When they do talk, the goal is to create in the minds of women someone who they are not. Silent Deceivers are so skillful at this tactic that the women normally do not discover the truth until after their feelings and heart are involved and they are in love. Because of the effectiveness of the shrewd and clever way in which the Silent Deceiver presents himself, women initially say, "I have met my soul mate. He is God-sent. He is a gentleman. He's polite, kind, sincere, giving, trustworthy, forgiving, lovable, loving, and precious." They really believe that he is their dream boy. To their surprise, not only is he none of those things, he's usually their worst nightmare. The poem below may illustrate the need for women to take it slowly when embarking on a new relationship. Remember, it is much easier to control your emotions before you are sexually involved than it is to control them after your mate has turned you on sexually.

The poem below tells part of the sad saga of the results of this impersonator.

Chapter 6: The Silent Deceiver Player

My Dream Boy

He came to me in noiseless splendor
With a bronze and mahogany veneer
His majesty the king stood confident and bold
While his body screamed
"I'm the man without fear!"

I said to myself
"Who is this man?" A mortal sculpture to behold
And why does he stand above all other men
As the authentic pot of gold?

He sparkled and glittered from head to toe
In effortless motions of chic
A velvet voice with magnificent words
"O yes, this is the man I must keep!"

My dream boy I thought had finally arrived
What joy and jubilation I felt
Don't wake me from this phenomenal sleep
'Cause I'm basking in his galaxy of wealth

Dream is a powerful five-letter word
A reverie mental ploy
The games it plays with the human consciousness
Cause the soul to believe it's a toy

Other five-letter words magnify the dream
To bring realism to the mind
They testify and solidify the meaning of a dream
And nullify the question why?

Five-letter words like honor and sweet
And poise and sense and loyal
Noble, value, trust, and adore
My dream boy was stepping on sacred soil

Five-letter words like worth and heart
And charm and magic and proud
Class, clean, valor, and ideal
This suave, smooth man would not be bowed

Five-letter words like award and exalt
And focus and right and prize
Skill, grace, valid, and taste
He was completely detached from any disguise

Five-letter words like light and truth
And power and evoke and crown
I was swimming in an ocean of make believe
Get a grip on yourself or you'll drown

An anchor of reality was sent my way
A navigator to test the tides
As I rode the Pacific fighting currents and waves
The Holy Spirit spoke and commenced to confide

Your dream boy is not a dream boy at all
His persona is all a fake
Awake yourself to the anointed air
Your dream boy is really a nightmare

This is the cruel truth of the Silent Deceiver Player. The lesson to learn from this player is: Who you think you see may be the exact opposite of who he is!

Below is a survey for the males to determine if you are a Silent Deceiver. Take your time and re-discover yourself.

ARE YOU A SILENT DECEIVER PLAYER?

Directions: Answer the following questions honestly and find out if you are a Silent Deceiver.

1) I never let my women know who I really am.

1. Strongly Agree
2. Agree
3. Somewhat Agree
4. Disagree
5. Strongly Disagree

2) I tell women little or nothing about myself.

1. Strongly Agree
2. Agree
3. Somewhat Agree
4. Disagree
5. Strongly Disagree

3) I like to rule my women.

1. Strongly Agree
2. Agree
3. Somewhat Agree
4. Disagree
5. Strongly Disagree

4) I like to control my women.

1. Strongly Agree
2. Agree
3. Somewhat Agree

4. Disagree
5. Strongly Disagree

5) I like to dominate my women.

1. Strongly Agree
2. Agree
3. Somewhat Agree
4. Disagree
5. Strongly Disagree

6) I like to manipulate my women.

1. Strongly Agree
2. Agree
3. Somewhat Agree
4. Disagree
5. Strongly Disagree

7) I try to hide my inadequacies from my women.

1. Strongly Agree
2. Agree
3. Somewhat Agree
4. Disagree
5. Strongly Disagree

8) My women don't know this but my heart is not right.

1. Strongly Agree
2. Agree
3. Somewhat Agree
4. Disagree
5. Strongly Disagree

9) I don't know how to love my women in a healthy way.

1. Strongly Agree
2. Agree
3. Somewhat Agree
4. Disagree
5. Strongly Disagree

10) I don't know how to like my women in a healthy way.

1. Strongly Agree
2. Agree
3. Somewhat Agree
4. Disagree
5. Strongly Disagree

11) I am a phony when it comes to the person I present to women.

1. Strongly Agree
2. Agree
3. Somewhat Agree
4. Disagree
5. Strongly Disagree

12) My women don't know that I'm not secure like I appear to be.

1. Strongly Agree
2. Agree
3. Somewhat Agree
4. Disagree
5. Strongly Disagree

13) My women don't know that I'm not strong like I appear to be.

1. Strongly Agree
2. Agree
3. Somewhat Agree
4. Disagree
5. Strongly Disagree

14) I hide from my own truth.

1. Strongly Agree
2. Agree
3. Somewhat Agree
4. Disagree
5. Strongly Disagree

15) I never let women know what my motives are.

1. Strongly Agree
2. Agree
3. Somewhat Agree
4. Disagree
5. Strongly Disagree

16) Even my kindness toward women is deceitful.

1. Strongly Agree
2. Agree
3. Somewhat Agree
4. Disagree
5. Strongly Disagree

17) Whatever I do for my women is a setup to get them to do what I want.

1. Strongly Agree
2. Agree
3. Somewhat Agree
4. Disagree
5. Strongly Disagree

18) My major purpose in relationships is to fool my women.

1. Strongly Agree
2. Agree
3. Somewhat Agree
4. Disagree
5. Strongly Disagree

19) I deceive women so I can get my way by any means necessary.

1. Strongly Agree
2. Agree
3. Somewhat Agree
4. Disagree
5. Strongly Disagree

Do you want to know your score? Below is the breakdown for rating and scoring yourself. Enjoy the exercise.

Rating Scale
Strongly Agree = 5 points
Agree = 4 points
Somewhat Agree = 3 points
Disagree = 2 points
Strongly Disagree = 1 point

Scoring Scale
90-100 = You are definitely a Silent Deceiver.
89-80 = You are a Silent Deceiver.
79-70 = You may be a Silent Deceiver.
69-60 = You are not a Silent Deceiver.
59 and below = You are definitely not a Silent Deceiver.

What did your score reveal to you? Were you surprised or did you already know everything that was revealed? I hope you enjoyed the exercise.

Women, it's your turn. Below is the survey to determine if you are involved with a Silent Deceiver Player. Take your time to complete it.

ARE YOU IN AN INTIMATE SEXUAL RELATIONSHIP WITH A SILENT DECEIVER PLAYER?

Directions: Answer the following questions honestly and find out if you are dating a Silent Deceiver.

1) My man hides his real self from me.

1. Strongly Agree
2. Agree
3. Somewhat Agree
4. Disagree
5. Strongly Disagree

2) My man tells me very little about himself.

1. Strongly Agree
2. Agree

3. Somewhat Agree
4. Disagree
5. Strongly Disagree

3) My man likes to control me.

1. Strongly Agree
2. Agree
3. Somewhat Agree
4. Disagree
5. Strongly Disagree

4) My man likes to rule me.

1. Strongly Agree
2. Agree
3. Somewhat Agree
4. Disagree
5. Strongly Disagree

5) My man likes to dominate me.

1. Strongly Agree
2. Agree
3. Somewhat Agree
4. Disagree
5. Strongly Disagree

6) My man likes to manipulate me.

1. Strongly Agree
2. Agree
3. Somewhat Agree
4. Disagree
5. Strongly Disagree

7) My man tries to hide his inadequacies from me.

1. Strongly Agree
2. Agree
3. Somewhat Agree
4. Disagree
5. Strongly Disagree

8) My man thinks I don't know that his heart is not right.

1. Strongly Agree
2. Agree
3. Somewhat Agree
4. Disagree
5. Strongly Disagree

9) My man does not know how to love me in a healthy way.

1. Strongly Agree
2. Agree
3. Somewhat Agree
4. Disagree
5. Strongly Disagree

10) My man does not know how to like me in a healthy way.
1. Strongly Agree
2. Agree
3. Somewhat Agree
4. Disagree
5. Strongly Disagree

11) I believe my man is a phony.
1. Strongly Agree
2. Agree
3. Somewhat Agree
4. Disagree
5. Strongly Disagree

12) I believe my man is a fake.
1. Strongly Agree
2. Agree
3. Somewhat Agree
4. Disagree
5. Strongly Disagree

13) I believe my man is insecure.
1. Strongly Agree
2. Agree
3. Somewhat Agree
4. Disagree
5. Strongly Disagree

14) I believe that my man is weak.
1. Strongly Agree
2. Agree
3. Somewhat Agree
4. Disagree
5. Strongly Disagree

15) I believe my man hides from his own truth.
1. Strongly Agree
2. Agree
3. Somewhat Agree
4. Disagree
5. Strongly Disagree

16) My man tries to hide from me his motives which would explain his behavior.
1. Strongly Agree
2. Agree
3. Somewhat Agree
4. Disagree
5. Strongly Disagree

17) My man's kind gestures are based on deceit.
1. Strongly Agree
2. Agree

3. Somewhat Agree
4. Disagree
5. Strongly Disagree

18) When my man does something for me, it's really to set me up so I can do something really big for him.

1. Strongly Agree
2. Agree
3. Somewhat Agree
4. Disagree
5. Strongly Disagree

19) I believe my man's major purpose in this relationship is to fool me.

1. Strongly Agree
2. Agree
3. Somewhat Agree
4. Disagree
5. Strongly Disagree

20) My man deceives me so that he can get his way by any means necessary.

1. Strongly Agree
2. Agree
3. Somewhat Agree
4. Disagree
5. Strongly Disagree

Here are your rating and scoring scales.

Rating Scale
Strongly Agree = 5 points
Agree = 4 points
Somewhat Agree = 3 points
Disagree = 2 points
Strongly Disagree = l point

Scoring Scale
90-100 = You are definitely in a relationship with a Silent Deceiver.
89-80 = You are in a relationship with a Silent Deceiver.
79-70 = You may be in a relationship with a Silent Deceiver.
69-60 = You are not in a relationship with a Silent Deceiver.
59 and below = You are definitely not in a relationship with a Silent Deceiver.

Chapter 7

The Philophobic Player

I'm as smooth as silk
As suave as an aristocrat
When a woman walks past me
I tip my fedora hat

I put the G in genteel
The WB in well-bred
I'm so polite and polished
Ladies want to lock me up
In their passionate lovers' bed

They have not a clue
That underneath my facade
Is a man without a love emotion
And a heart that perpetrates a fraud

I have no affection or fondness
For any woman I meet
The thought of a loving relationship
Makes cold blood run from my head to my feet

I still have relationships
With two or three women at the same time
They provide me with a safety net
And a "do not disturb my feelings" sign

This love "thang" woman seek
And very few ever find
Is what I try to avoid
For me, it's all about
I, Me, and Mine

"Philo" What?

During the course of the time spent writing this book, I held many focus groups on each chapter. The goal was to get a sense of the groups' reaction to the typologies for players. Whenever the Philophobic Player was discussed, the comments from the audience varied dramatically from those at other sessions. When I mentioned the term "philophobic", the following responses were virtually the same at each session: "'Philo' what?" "'Philo' who?" "What does that mean?" "I've never heard that word." I explained to them that a Philophobic is a person who has a fear of falling in love, being in love, and staying in love. Philophobia is a deep fear of love and intimacy in relationships. This fear is constant and intense. Different participants in the group then responded, "There are people who really don't love?" "I thought everybody loved." "Who are these people?" "How can you recognize them?" My retort was, "Yes, there are people who don't love in intimate sexual relationships. They don't have a desire to love. Given their fear of love, they very well may be incapable of loving in an intimate, sexual relationship. In this case, Philophobics are men who fear romantic love. Another interesting characteristic about these men that is also like the other Betrayers is that in their incognito persona, they do not afford women the ability to recognize them—at least not initially."

A female inquired, "How can a woman know that a man is philophobic? What are the signs?" My response was, "You can't, especially during the early stage or even later stages of the relationship. Time, keen observations, inquiry, insight, and a very critical and analytical intellect may allow you to unravel the web of the Philophobic. After you apply these skills to determine the status of his *love emotion*, it is not a given that you will discover he is philophobic." Upon hearing this revelation, the group was stunned on the one hand and eager to know more about these enigmatic individuals on the other.

"Philo" Who?

Philophobic Players can aptly be described as mercurial, superficial, and merciless in their relationships with women. A simple sentence that may help women have a better sense of philophobics is: They are shallow, wobbly men who have no pity on women who fall in love with them. They can *appear* to be the personification of chivalry, or cold as the continent of Antarctica, or sweet as cotton candy, or mean as Scrooge, or stilted as soldiers guarding Buckingham Palace in England, or as flexible in behavior as contortionists are in body movements, or as lovable as huggable teddy bears, or all of the above. If they wore a sign on their chests stating, "Warning! Enter at your own risk," women could be alerted to the need to "abort the approach". Well, they don't wear a sign. Therefore, women are on their own in figuring out who they really are. They will put the movie *The Usual Suspects* to shame. They can fool women from all walks of life. Women can be as smart as a genius or as green as Johnson's grass, or as street as concrete on a city expressway, or as sexual as a nymphomaniac, or as skillful as a top-of-the-line journeyman, or as cunning as a con artist who is slick as grease, and still make the Philophobic's "I fooled you" list.

Chapter 7: The Philophobic Player

What is known of these predatory men at this time is that their behavior is learned, cultivated, and based on a personal choice. It is that plain and simple.

Love Who? Love What? Love How?

Love is an emotion that has been embraced, celebrated, encouraged, and demonstrated since the beginning of time. It is the most Googled word on the Internet. Religious leaders remind us that God is love. Psychologists write about the power of love in the development of emotionally healthy children. Marriage counselors stress the importance of love in healthy, meaningful spousal relationships. Literary writers have amassed prose and poetry expressing the dynamics of love. Romantic love means to Philophobics what *Love* means in the scoring of a tennis match: Zero! However, just because the Philophobic Player is uninterested in romantic love, do not assume that he does not love himself, or at least he thinks he does.

Narcissism, the love of oneself, is associated with philophobia. The love at the healthy end of the narcissistic continuum is a positive and useful love. It is the love that lays the foundation for the building of self-confidence and self-esteem. It is the love that allows an individual to have an I am, I will, I must, and I can, type attitude, philosophy, and behavior. At the other end, it may manifest in NPD, Narcissistic Personality Disorder (DSM-IV, 2000). At this end, the love of self is viewed as manipulative, two-faced, conniving, deceitful, fake, and egocentric. Those closest to individuals with a NPD are their most likely victims. The demeanor of persons with a NPD will vacillate from charming, humble, likable, and polite, especially in public, to rude, abrasive, obnoxious, pretentious, and aggressive in private. They misuse the kindness of others. They exaggerate their accomplishments. They project an image that suggests that even though they are superior to and better than others, they are envious of others' achievements. Although their egos may be weak and fragile, they will act tough and emotionally detached about whatever is going on around them. They are attention seekers. They lie a lot about who they really are and what they really want.

Remember, in romantic love relationships, these men are mercurial in character. Mercurial Philophobic men build relationships on unstable grounds. I describe these relationships as *the Mercurial Facade*. By now you may be asking, "Do some Philophobic Players suffer from NPD?" The answer is an unequivocal, *Yes!* Moreover, the *Diagnostic and Statistical Manual of Mental Disorder* (DSM-IV, 2000) indicates that

"a NPD is 50%-75% more prevalent in men than women". The Philophobic Player with a NPD may answer the questions about the who, what, and how of love in the following way: Who I love is me. What I love are my possessions I own that I choose to love. And how I love is my business and my business only.

When One Time Is Too Many

Have you had life encounters that were so devastating, you vowed to never revisit them again in your lifetime, even if you lived to be 120 years old? Philophobics have. Their vows were just the opposite of wedding vows. They vowed to develop, embrace, and forever hold tightly to and live by an anti-romantic love mentality and behavior platform. Their tenacious belief in this mentality may cause others to think that they *never* loved anyone romantically. Such is not the case. Actually, each one of them admitted to being in love at least once, no more than twice, before becoming Philophobic. Their recall was laced with bitterness and regret. They were so adamant about never loving again romantically, you would have thought that the love relationship left them without a leg, an arm, a foot, paralyzed from neck down, or with a terminal disease. They spoke negatively about themselves, admitting to being out of control during the relationship and resenting it. When they mentioned women with whom they were sexually involved, they were really low-rated. They were called almost everything but saints. One Philophobic stated, "Some women will make you not want to have a woman." These Philophobics claimed that the women set them up. The women were no good. They tricked them into falling in love with them. They weren't about nothing anyway. Then, they concluded that they never, ever want to love again.

The Love of *My* Branches That Fell from the Roots of *My* Tree

Philophobics were unanimous in their expressions of love toward their offspring. They were also quick to brag about their children's educational and career accomplishments. It did appear that the expressions of love toward their offspring far outweighed the demonstrations of love and the frequency with which they saw them, talked to them, and spent quality time with them. In two cases where the men were divorced, they admitted, though reluctantly, that they were emotionally absent from their children. Both attempted to compensate for this by buying them material things. They used their faulty relationship with the mothers of their children as the reason for their lack of quality time spent with and strong emotional attachment to their children. Philophobic men without children had no desire to become fathers. The Philophobics stated that their children were their treasured gifts; but the love of *the roots* far outweighed the love of the branches.

Chapter 7: The Philophobic Player

The Family and Friends Love Tree Connection

A Philophobic shared a story with the group that occurred with his parents and 10 siblings at a family reunion. He said everyone in his family was sitting around laughing and talking about family stories. One of the stories involved the love one brother showed to another during the brother's illness. This Philophobic brother said he stood up and proclaimed, "Do you know who I love? Do you know who I really love? I love me. That's who I love." Afterward, he said one of his sisters told him that she just knew he was going to say that he loved his parents, especially since they were there. He didn't see anything wrong with what he said. He told his sister that he does love his parents, but he loves himself more.

Philophobics claim that they are not afraid of loving their family members. Since Philophobics did not choose their family members, they admit that they do not like all of them but they do love them in a familial way. They believe that their family love tree connection is no different from relationships non-Philophobics have with their family members. They admit to caring for, sharing, and "hanging out" with family members, as well as giving of themselves emotionally, financially, socially, and psychologically to them. They added that friends, on the other hand, are selected based on a sense of camaraderie, with similarities in values, personalities, and goals. But they basically give of themselves to their friends the same way they give to their family members. Based on these disclosures, the questions I asked the Philophobics were: "What is it about the love of family and friends that does not incite fear in your hearts? And, why do you feel you can maintain your power, control, and domination in family and friendship relations and lose it in romantic relationships?" Below is a summary of their most salient responses.

- Sex is not involved.
- Family and friend relationships don't cloud my judgment.
- A romantic love relationship is too time-consuming.
- A romantic relationship is too distracting; I lose sight of important things in my life.
- I become too possessive and controlling.
- I didn't like myself when I was in love.
- Women play too many games.
- I don't want to be hurt.
- A romantic relationship is too much of a power struggle; and what if I don't win?
- I feel too vulnerable.
- I don't ever want to feel the pain I felt when a woman told me that she had found someone else.
- You can't trust women with your feelings.

- I'm still trying to find out who I am; I don't need to get involved in an intimate relationship. [The males who said this were 43 and 47 years old.]
- I want all of my freedom, and a woman takes your freedom away.
- Women want to control you and tell you what to do.
- I had to admit to myself that sex weakens me, and I don't like to feel weak.
- Nine times out of 10, my family and friends will have my back. A woman will probably leave me in the lurch.
- What if I'm all in love and the woman does not love me back?
- I don't want to marry, so why should I fall in love?
- I don't want to care that deeply for a woman.
- I would be too jealous.
- I'm afraid of commitment.
- I don't want to share myself like that with a woman.
- I'm just scared as hell of feeling sexual and intimate love for a woman.
- I don't want to lose my balance.

These comments indicate that the fear of intimate sexual loving relationships manifests in four principal ways: 1) Fear of being hurt, 2) Fear of experiencing the pain that may result from that hurt, 3) Fear of losing control of one's emotions, and 4) Fear of the absence of power and dominion over one's total self. If one were to develop a formula for identifying Philophobics based on the above mentioned responses, it may look like this:

The Fear of Hurt + The Fear of Pain + The Fear of Losing Control + The Fear of Losing Power and Domination = A Philophobic

The moral of this story is: Fear is something to be *feared*!

The Love of Clothes and Accessories

Most Philophobics enjoy their material possessions. They like acquiring them and they love sporting them whenever they are in the mood to be "swanky and splashy." They are usually well-coordinated with what's on their heads, their backs, their legs, their feet, their wrists, their fingers, and what's around their necks. They claim that they don't let material possessions define them. They believe that they make their "material things" look good because they are wearing them. As one Philophobic stated, "My clothes don't define me. I define my clothes." While they enjoy wearing quality and designer apparel, they tend not to be big-time spenders. As a matter of fact, they pride themselves on finding bargains and then bragging about what good shoppers they are. If you see them, especially at an affair or at a gala event, some people will describe their appearance in one of the following ways:

"He looks like Mr. Dapper Dan." "He's as clean as the Board of Health." "He is exquisitely dressed." "He is dressed to the nines." "He needs to be on the cover of *Esquire.*" They usually make women do a double take when they see them. These men look very appealing and inviting. However, you may recall the *beware* warning sign mentioned earlier. Make sure it stays in your memory bank in case a Philophobic Player has targeted you as his next victim.

Although most Philophobics will follow this dress pattern, there are some who will not. Therefore, consider several characteristics of these men before drawing a final conclusion.

The Home and Furnishings: What's Love Got to Do with Them?

Although some Philophobics admitted that they were lacking in their domestic skills or just not into keeping a neat and tidy home, their abode was described as average to above average in appearance. Their furnishings may have left a lot to be desired, to say the least. I recall this particular Philophobic who described a situation that occurred when he invited a woman to his home after he had taken her to dinner. He said that as he drove in his driveway, she complimented him on how nice his house was. He knew her opinion would change once she saw the inside. He noted that her first reaction was silence. He then broke the silence by saying, "I'm not really into furniture." When they walked in the bedroom, she noticed that the bed was without a headboard. She asked, "Where is your headboard?" He replied, "I don't need a headboard to do what I do in the bed. Do you?" After they had sex, she asked him if he had gone to the Salvation Army to purchase his furniture. He said he could not do anything but laugh because she wasn't the first woman to say that. In fact, he said one woman asked him if he bought the furniture from a Goodwill thrift store. Another told him that she had some furniture she could give him. Still another asked him, "How can you live in this nice home and not buy any decent furniture?" He told her that it didn't bother him because he was rarely home. He admitted that furniture was never a priority for him. He also noted that regardless of women's complaints about his furniture, they continued to see him until he was tired of them. He stated that each one played the MacArthur role—"I shall return"—and returned again, and again, and again…

One Philophobic stated that he lives in a very nice gated apartment complex. He noted that the women were always surprised when they entered his two-bedroom apartment and found a billiard table in the living room and a small leather sofa, bar, and four bar stools in the dining room. He said that he had a small kitchen table with two chairs in the tiny kitchen. When the women complained about the location of the billiard table and the cluttered kitchen, he would tell them that his apartment was set up for him and him only. He went on to say that women would complain about the poor quality and age of his bed linen, though that never stopped them from coming to bed. One woman, he said, was so tired of sleeping on the same old, faded sheets when she spent the night that she bought him three sets of 600-thread-count Martha Stewart sheets. "That's what she was supposed to do if the sheets bothered her. They didn't bother me," he proclaimed.

Remember, females, the Philophobic Player is into his wants, needs, and desires and not the wishes of the women with whom he is involved.

I Love My Automobile

Most men are known to have a special relationship with their vehicles. The Philophobic not only has a special relationship with his automobile, he loves it. He sees it as an extension of his personality and who he is. He is usually so particular about it that he will refuse valet parking rather than allow someone else to drive it, unless it is impossible to park it any other way. He will wash it, buff it, wax it, vacuum it, and Windex it until it shines like new money. Do not change the CD. Do not change the channel on the radio. Do not move the seat. Do not move the mirrors. And do not leave paper anywhere in it. These are the same men who admitted to having an unkempt house with antiquated furniture. Yet their cars are immaculate. And they are usually luxury cars, not older than one-three years, unless they are cars that are kept for vintage value. These are examples of selective priority for the love of material things. One Philophobic contrasted the love and care he gives his automobile with what he gives to the woman with whom he is in a relationship. He admitted that if the women knew the difference, they would choose to be his vehicle. As another Philophobic put it, "Women ought to be like automobiles. As long as you treat your vehicle right, you can drive it for years and years. No sooner than you treat women right, they want to own you. They want you to spend all your time with them. They want you to call them all the time and tell them what you're doing. They will turn a smooth ride in a car into one that is as bumpy as bumper cars on a carousel."

The Love of God—the Love of a Supreme Being

Who hasn't heard Biblical sayings such as, "God is love," "For God so loved the world..." "Faith, hope and charity (love), but the greatest of these is love"? The Philophobics admitted to knowing about each one. In spite of the Philophobics' fear of love in an intimate, sexual relationship, none of them attempted to refute or contradict these statements. It was also interesting that none of them saw themselves as an atheist or agnostic. All believed in God or a Supreme Being, or a Creator. Although most of them did not practice any formalized religion, they considered themselves spiritual persons. There was an obvious connection to them and what they referred to as religious, spiritual, or gospel music. They were quite familiar with gospel artists, past and present, such as James Cleveland, Tennessee Ernie Ford, Shirley Caesar, Amy Grant, Kirk Franklin, and BeBe and CeCe Winans.

From the Philophobics' point of view, you can love God and spiritual music and have no desire to engage in love in a romantic, sexual, and intimate relationship. Philophobics have no problem separating the two.

The Philophobic Players' Richter Scale

A Richter scale, named after the renowned American seismologist Charles F. Richter, measures the conditions and seismic disturbances of earthquakes from 1.5 at the low end of detectable movements to 8.5 at the high end. Like earthquakes, all Philophobics are not measured alike. Their effect on women with whom they have been intimately and sexually involved has a range similar to that of the Richter scale. Those women at or close to the low end of the emotional Richter scale, caused by an intimate sexual relationship with a Philophobic, suffer from the release of floods of water through the outpouring of tears, tremors of depression, a landslide of misplaced passion, and a shaken human infrastructure that manifests itself in feelings of dejection, rejection, estrangement, detachment, aloneness, and loneliness. The women whose experiences with a Philophobic catapulted them at or near the emotionally devastated high end of the emotional Richter scale sustained a deformed sense of self-worth, a collapsed physiology that is evident by difficulty falling asleep, staying asleep, loss of appetite or uncontrollable food consumption, and the onslaught of allergies causing excessive sneezing, coughing, and runny nose. The women who received the highest level of the emotional wrath that was equivalent to an emotional human tsunami bore the pains of distrust, betrayal, and tidal waves of feelings of sadness, helplessness, hopelessness, powerlessness, and worthlessness. The emotional aftermath of their distressful relationship with a Philophobic ended in an emotional eruption that almost decimated them psychologically, physically, mentally, and socially.

The methods used to hide the motives that explain philophobic behavior have their variance, too. The philophobic seismic relationships are highlighted below. These categories by no means exhaust all Philophobic types. They do serve to expose some of the human climatic disturbances that result in philophobic earthquakes, hurricanes, and tornadoes.

The Quicksand Quackster

You probably have never seen the words *quicksand* and *quackster* side by side, representing anything, or defining anybody.

Can you imagine the usage of these words to describe a type of Philophobic Player? To more fully understand this type of behavior in Philophobics, let's take a look at quicksand. Western movies commonly depict someone getting stuck in quicksand. If someone were in close proximity to the person stuck, that person would extend a hand or a stick for the person stuck to hold on to in hopes of pulling the victim to safety. Those watching the movies who don't understand quicksand may ask, "How did the person get in it? Didn't the person know it was quicksand? Aren't there signs to alert a person to the dangers of quicksand? Having been stuck in quicksand once, is there any guarantee that the person will never fall victim to quicksand again?" These penetrating questions not only get at the crux of inquiry regarding quicksand, but they also speak to the dangers of romantic involvement with a Philophobic who is an impostor and perpetrates a fraud. Simply put, he is flaky because his foundation is so shaky.

Just how shaky is Mr. Flaky? Believe it or not, he is so flaky, he defies Sir Isaac Newton's Third Law of Motion. At this point, you know that is flaky, but you are probably asking: What does Newton's theory have to do with philophobics, anyway? How can this type of Philophobic make Newton's law null and void? Simply put, Newton's Action-Reaction Third Law of Motion (as cited in Resnick, Halliday, & Krane, 1992) says, *For every action, there's an equal and opposite reaction.* From Newton's point of view, a body remains in a state of rest unless some external force disturbs it. Note this: Newton, a masterful and scholarly physicist, astronomer, and mathematician, also says that when some outside force disturbs the body, the change in motion is proportional to and in the same direction as the force that was applied to it.

The reason quicksand does not support Newton's Third Law of Motion is because quicksand gives the appearance of being in a state of rest. Put another way, it gives the appearance of being solid, when in fact it is not. Therefore, it is a non-Newtonian fluid that is not in a state of rest, even when nothing or no one is disturbing it. As powerful and as meaningful as Newton's Third Law of Motion is, one of the conditions that does not fit this law is quicksand. Remember, quicksand is easy to get in and hard to get out. In fact, it can take you under.

Quacks are mentioned as part of the dark side of the medical field. As illustrated by the sentiment, "He's nothing but a quack. He doesn't know anything about medicine." The reference is to a person who wants others to think he has acquired a vast amount of medical knowledge. He may even claim to have a medical degree. A quack and a quackster have similar characteristics. They are pretenders and counterfeiters. In the context of philophobia, these frauds claim to be in search of legitimate romantic, meaningful relationships. The truth is, their conversation and behavior are fraudulent, and thus, they are as unreliable as quicksand would be if a wrestling ring were placed on it with 20 wrestlers, each weighing 350-550 pounds. You get the message, don't you?

Heartless Hedonist

This Heartless Hedonist comes into your life gift wrapped in a ball of contradictions. On the one hand, he is unemotional, callous, coldhearted, and unsympathetic. On the other hand, he is pleasure-seeking. He truly believes that pleasure is the highest good. He thinks it is his moral duty to fulfill this highest good through the pursuit of pleasure. The question becomes: How is he defining pleasure? His ultimate pleasure is at the expense of another person's sufferings. He is so hell-bent on self-indulgence, self-satisfaction, and self-gratification that he will literally inflict pain on women. This helps him achieve his level of desired joy and bliss. The contradiction that lies within this person who is devoid of feelings of affection in a sexual intimate relationship and yet is pleasure-seeking can be best described as *The Epigrammatic Effect.* He presents himself as kind, caring, and warmhearted, but in actuality he is cruel and uncompassionate. On top of that, he plays a game that can be called *blaming the victims.* To him, it is the women's fault that they didn't have enough sense to discern his true self and his real motives. It is in this vein that he sees himself as blameless and free of scorn. By now you may be asking: Since he doesn't love romantically, how does he make love to the women with whom he is involved? The answer is simple: he doesn't. He has sex with them. The sex act is all about his sexual pleasures and what the women can do to satisfy him. As one Philophobic puts it so succinctly, "I only need women to fulfill my sexual needs." He is fully aware of his one-sided sexual mentality. Therefore, he seeks women who will let him have his way with them.

If Philophobics were asked, "Qui Bono? (Who benefits?)," they will quickly acknowledge that they and they alone are the benefactors in their sexual relationship. These men are not shy about speaking on their sexual goals. With pride in his voice, one Philophobic described his sexual relationships with women as a *freak mission.* "I only look for freaks; I prefer diabolical freaks; they'll do almost anything; just let them get their freak on and they will put on a freak show you won't forget." Still another said, "I use some sex acts to lock down their mind. Once I find them, I f—k the dog s—t out of them. That allows me to have full control of them." He added, "I've sent some women to the edge and I've sent other women over the edge." This description was used to indicate how he used sex acts to cause women to lose their mental stability. These statements were made proudly, without any sign of emotional trepidation, as though their biggest orgasm came from the mental destruction they caused to women.

One Philophobic had a most interesting explanation about his sexual behavior. He admitted to *fearing the power of the vagina.* Using the slang word for vagina that begins with a "p" and ends with a "y", this man talked about the time he spent at the video store viewing and then purchasing pornographic videos. He saw the sexual gratification of watching porno sex as the safest method to achieve sexual satisfaction without any emotional attachment with women. Upon hearing this explanation, I asked, "Would you classify yourself as voyeuristic?" He replied, "Yes, and what's wrong with that? I enjoy looking at her vagina but I don't want my penis to ever penetrate a vagina again. It's too risky. I could lose control of my emotions and the woman can take control of me. That happened to me one time and I'm not gonna let it happen again." I raised the following question: "Does this mean that you have no physical sexual contact with women?" His response was, "No. She can spank me and she can let me spank her. I like that." My next question was, "What type women will let you engage in these types of sexual acts that demonstrate a lack of affection and romantic love?" His reply was, "You would be surprised at the women who have no problem with this type of sex. I had a woman who was 76 years old [he was 53 at the time]. Anything I asked her to do, she did it. She was so glad to have a man in her life, and a young man at that, she didn't care that I didn't love her and would never love her. Plus, I didn't treat her badly. I was nice to her. If her kids needed something or if she needed something, I would help her if I could. We had a good arrangement."

When asked if he thought he would ever change and consider a committed relationship, he gave the following response, without hesitation: "No, never, because commitment is enslavement and I'm not about to be enslaved. I know I will stay the way I am because *there is too much sin in me*." This Philophobic perfected the art and skill of being a Philophobic to such a high level, he had it down to a science. If such a science were to be established, a logical name for it probably may be "Philophobiology". It would be defined as the scientific study of behavior that is anti-romance, anti-love, and fearful of the love emotion in intimate, sexual relationships. Can you imagine what these studies might reveal?

The Evil Egomaniac

Have you ever met a male who was in a relationship with himself? He thinks no one else is good enough for him. He suffers from swell-headedness, arrogance, and vainness. He is also devilish, wicked, distressful, and harmful. Well, meet Mr. Evil Egomaniac. His grandiose view of himself makes him believe that he can get any woman he wants. If you go out to a club to dance and socialize, he's the one standing against the wall waiting for the women to rush him, start a conversation with him, buy him a drink, and ask him for a dance. When they rush to him and approach him, he acts like he's annoyed by their aggressiveness, although on the inside, he's gloating and thinking to himself that if they were lucky enough to get him, he would be the best thing that ever happened to them. Bragging on his irresistible demeanor, one Philophobic put it this way: "All I have to do is go to a club and the women come running. Sometimes I indulge them with flattery and tell them how good they look and what I would like to do to them sexually. Other times, I just ignore them. It all depends on my mood."

Egomaniacs don't just hang out at clubs. Some are good church-going men who serve on trustee boards, deacon boards, and usher boards. Believe it or not, some are also clerics in the pulpit. This group of egomaniacs uses their positions in the church to promote a false image that is laced with: I am decent. I am a good catch. I am seeking a committed relationship. I am legitimate. I am trustworthy. I want a woman to love. And, I am looking for a wife. As one Philophobic stated, "The best place to go to find a woman who will take your s—t is in the church. They are the most desperate women. They will believe anything you tell them because they met you in the church. There are so many of them in the church, they try to do more for you because they know that competition is steep. They make good servants. They let me know that they are servants and not queens because a queen maintains her throne, even in the midst of a king."

During this discussion, a male who did not fit in this category agreed with the above explanation. His agreement was based on the perception women have about leaders in the church. "Women see them as a cut above the rest of the men. That's why they think they are good men. They need to remember that *devils dress up and go to church, too.*"

The moral of the Evil Egomaniac's story is: If a man has to flaunt his self-importance, just how important is he?

The Debonair Defrauder

Veneer, in the interior design profession, is an exterior covering. In the case of the Debonair Defrauder, it is a disguise. It is window dressing. It is the thin, outer layer of a lie. It is a false front. It is a misleading image. More often than not, women who need to be acutely aware of men who varnish their outward appearance to woo women are the very ones who ignore it. Since men are fully aware of this oversight, they dress to create a picture of themselves in a decorative frame that appeals to these women. It is clear to these men that being well-mannered and well-groomed are most appealing to most women. The Debonair Defrauder understands this type of female thinking, and as a result of this understanding, he adopts the motto: *I dress to deflect.*

His goal is to divert women's attention away from his true motives. He believes that if women become enthralled with his vitality and suave demeanor, they will not recognize him for who he really is—a con man, a double-dealer, and a flimflammer. As one Debonair Defrauder explained, "Women are shallow. They get turned on and turned out by superficial stuff." With this knowledge, he masterfully drapes himself in "old-school gentleman" behavior. He will greet a woman with a smile. When it comes to taking her out on a date, he arrives at her home on time or slightly early. He compliments her on her appearance, whether she deserves it or not. Before leaving, he makes sure her home is secure. He opens the car door for her and takes her by her arm to assist her as she gets in the car. If she's wearing a coat, he will make sure that her coat is neatly tucked in the car. When they arrive at the place where he is taking her, he will make sure that he is situated in front of her so he can open the door with grace and aplomb. He will take her coat and look for the coatroom or coat closet to make sure that her wrap is securely hung. What woman who is looking for a gentleman wouldn't be impressed by this show of chivalry? Most women would be in a state of euphoria. Women and some men who witness this behavior may turn their heads toward this man and take a second look. He truly will stand out in most crowds, or at least be admired by onlookers. Well, guess what? It's all a setup. It's all a part of his hoodwink and bamboozle plan to defraud the woman into believing that he is a *five-star* man among all men.

After he has successfully convinced her that the stars will always shine in her life as long as he is her man, he sets out to find two or three more women, and proceeds to persuade them that he is their manly Big Dipper and their well-bred Milky Way. As one Debonair Defrauder pointed out, "All you have to do is tell the woman that she is the light of your life and she will try to shine like the brightest star in the galaxy. Women love to be lied to. They don't want to know the truth about how you really feel about them. I just tell them what they want to hear and they do what I want them to do to me and for me. It ain't my fault that they can't be all that I say they are. They look in the mirror every day. If they lie to themselves and think that they are all that, what's wrong with me lying to them, too?"

By the time this man, who women define as their bright shining star, reveals to them that he is merely a dim flicker, they are weak in the knees, unstable in the head, bleeding in the heart, and deeply in love. They didn't have a clue that his masculine glamour and classy finesse were always about *him.* It was never about *them.*

The Arctic Agliophobic

The Arctic Agliophobic practices the art of the avoidance of emotional pain. The question this phobia raises is: Have you ever thought about what it's like to fear an intimate, sexual, romantic relationship because you thought it would have a painful ending? This type of fear explains agliophobia (Ramsey, 2010). It is caused by an external force (women) clashing with an internal anti-love disposition. These men are so afraid of the emotional pain emanating from a relationship that caused them misery and acute emotional discomfort that they insulate themselves with an impenetrable armor. Their fear of emotional pain is so intense that they can be described as a *quintuple philophobic*. They are philophobic to the fifth power. Their fears are five tiers in height. They suffer from:

A fear of intimacy
A fear of rejection
A fear of their partner leaving them
A fear of losing their self-identity
A fear of being out of control

These fears are a consequence of one or two past relationships they perceived as ending in turmoil and grief. They also see romantic love relationships as the reason for them becoming obsessive and possessive, thus losing their emotional balance and stability. When describing a relationship that presented him with great concern because he saw himself losing control of his emotions, an Agliophobic stated, "I was slipping. I was losing my sense of balance. This caused me to lose concentration on a lot of other things. I couldn't afford to let that happen, so I told the woman that I had lost interest in her and that she needed to move on." As you can discern from these statements and the actions taken, these fears were very real for him. His goal was to avoid pain from women and develop an Immune Efficiency System that will deny pain the right to enter his emotional system, thus rendering him emotionally *pain-free*. This avoidance is intentional, deliberate, and ongoing.

The scant literature on agliophobia has an interesting slant to it. It takes the position that people who have a fear of pain are seeking therapy, a remedy, a method of controlling it or at a higher level; they are seeking a cure. Symptoms of agliophobia are described as loss of appetite, difficulty falling asleep and staying asleep, breathlessness, problems thinking, shaking, nausea, and heart palpitations. The literature suggests that these individuals are looking for a way to relieve themselves of this anxiety disorder. These notions may hold true for other types of fear of pain, but they do not hold true for the Agliophobic who fears pain from romantic love.

First, Agliophobics are not interested in changing their reaction to their fear of romantic love. As one Agliophobic remarked: "I'm not going to change. I don't see no reason to change. I have worked hard to get to where I am. If women can't accept me for who I am, I tell them, so long, 'bye, see you." Still another noted, "I have manufactured a *new self* for myself and no woman is going to change it." With this attitude and the subsequent behavior that comes with it, you can imagine how cold and callous these men are in their relationships, if you can call them relationships. Their bitterness and hostility toward romantic relationships are unshakeable. They are beyond penetration. The Agliophobics are marked by a severe deficiency in emotional warmth and cordiality. Their emotional temperature is always below 32 degrees Fahrenheit, which is the freezing point. From this emotional point of view, they could occupy a space on the continent of Antarctica, or join the North and South Poles and fit right in. Their frosty, frigid, hardened, and unresponsive demeanor will allow them to comfortably survive and prosper in -50 degree Fahrenheit temperatures. Their heartless and cold-natured temperament makes them prime candidates for *a quintuplebypass.*

When one of the men was asked why he went to such lengths to escape romantic love, his comment was, "As a man, you don't ever want to feel vulnerable; even when you are vulnerable, you need to act like you're not." I followed that up with, "If that's the case, you never know who you really are, since you are constantly acting and playing a role that is not real." His response was, "After a while, you don't know the difference and you don't care."

In other words, he is so determined to maintain his anti-romantic love stance that he will risk losing himself, or he will, in actuality really lose himself, rather than open himself up to romantic love. I told this Agliophobic male that his desire to avoid *romantic love shock* was so strong that the formula for electricity came to mind as an explanation of his behavior from a physics point of view. Out of curiosity, he asked that I explain the connection.

The formula for electricity is:

V = I x R
V = Voltage
I = Current
and
R = Resistance

I told him that he saw romantic love as being so powerful (Current) he believed that he had to multiply the number of times he needed to resist it (Resistance); otherwise, he would be *electrocuted by romantic love*. He laughed and said, "Yes, that fits me; but I never would have explained it like that." The fear of being electrocuted by romantic love is a driving force that keeps Agliophobics the way they are. Therefore, to them, the thought of changing this fear is totally out of the question.

The Painless Predator

If you thought you had read about the pinnacle of philophobics when you read about the arctic agliophobic, you are wrong. Imagine men who have such an anti-romantic love attitude that their desire is to be completely incapable of experiencing pain from romantic love. That is, the avoidance of pain is not enough for them. As one painless predator put it, "I want to be like Superman. He never felt pain. That's who I want to be." Trying to get romantic love out of these men is like trying to get a basketball with no air in it to bounce. It will never happen. These men make no apology for their anti-romantic love sentiments.

Keep in mind that these painless predators still engage in male-female relationships. The manner in which they relate to women does not give any inkling that they desire to be emotionally pain free. They present themselves to women in such a way that it makes the women think that not only are they capable of loving, they are desirous of loving as well. They proceed from there to prey on women's emotions. They want women to love them and care about them. They set in motion a victimization game and use women to give them a false sense of self-worth and valuation. When one painless predator was asked why he did this to women, his retort was, "I like to see women fall apart. I like for them to ask me what else they can do to get my attention. What can they do to get me to show my love for them? I give them some song and dance story about what they are not doing and what they do that I don't like. I tell them to go back to their strategy room to try to figure out new ways to get my attention." I asked him if he felt badly about knowing that these women were fighting a losing battle. His response was, "Not at all. These are grown women. They ought to be able to tell by my behavior that I am not interested in them." I followed that question with, "Since you don't care about them, why do you get involved with them?" He proclaimed, "Sometimes I like the company of females, but that doesn't mean I want to love them."

This man's rationale for his behavior indicates insensitivity to the emotional feelings of women. It may also speak to emotional decay on his part. When I asked him if he thought that he was experiencing emotional decadence when it comes to romantic love, his response was, "I never thought about it like that, but if emotional decadence means that my romantic love emotion is dead, I would have to agree with you. It will stay dead. It will not be resurrected for no woman."

Females, he is who he is. What more can I say?

Men, you may not have heard about this concept, but now you know its meaning. Your answers to the following questions will let you know if you fit this type of player.

ARE YOU A PHILOPHOBIC PLAYER?

Directions: Answer the following questions honestly and find out if you are a Philophobic Player. Circle the number by the answer that best fits you.

1) My women believe that I am a gentleman.
1. Strongly Agree
2. Agree
3. Somewhat Agree
4. Disagree
5. Strongly Disagree

2) My women think I am a very secure man.
1. Strongly Agree
2. Agree
3. Somewhat Agree
4. Disagree
5. Strongly Disagree

3) My women think I really love myself.
1. Strongly Agree
2. Agree
3. Somewhat Agree
4. Disagree
5. Strongly Disagree

4) My women think I am a very confident man.
1. Strongly Agree
2. Agree
3. Somewhat Agree
4. Disagree
5. Strongly Disagree

5) My women don't know that I have a fear of loving.
1. Strongly Agree
2. Agree
3. Somewhat Agree
4. Disagree
5. Strongly Disagree

6) My women don't know that I fear falling in love.
1. Strongly Agree
2. Agree
3. Somewhat Agree
4. Disagree
5. Strongly Disagree

7) My women don't know that I fear being in love.
1. Strongly Agree
2. Agree
3. Somewhat Agree
4. Disagree
5. Strongly Disagree

8) My women don't know that I have relationships with two or more women so that I don't have to focus on one woman.
1. Strongly Agree
2. Agree
3. Somewhat Agree

4. Disagree
5. Strongly Disagree

9) My women don't know that my goal in intimate relationships is to protect my feelings.

1. Strongly Agree
2. Agree
3. Somewhat Agree
4. Disagree
5. Strongly Disagree

10) My women don't know that I'm incapable of loving.

1. Strongly Agree
2. Agree
3. Somewhat Agree
4. Disagree
5. Strongly Disagree

11) The women with whom I am in a sexual relationship don't realize that I don't care about them.

1. Strongly Agree
2. Agree
3. Somewhat Agree
4. Disagree
5. Strongly Disagree

12) The women with whom I am in a sexual relationship don't realize that I have no affection for them.

1. Strongly Agree
2. Agree
3. Somewhat Agree
4. Disagree
5. Strongly Agree

13) The women with whom I am in a sexual relationship don't realize that I have no fondness for them.

1. Strongly Agree
2. Agree
3. Somewhat Agree
4. Disagree
5. Strongly Disagree

14) The women with whom I am in a sexual relationship don't realize that I am only concerned about myself.

1. Strongly Agree
2. Agree
3. Somewhat Agree
4. Disagree
5. Strongly Disagree

15) My women think I really love them.

1. Strongly Agree
2. Agree
3. Somewhat Agree

4. Disagree
5. Strongly Disagree

16) My women confuse my ability to have sex with them with loving them.

1. Strongly Agree
2. Agree
3. Somewhat Agree
4. Disagree
5. Strongly Disagree

17) My women confuse my knowing how to treat them with loving them. There is a difference, at least, in my case.

1. Strongly Agree
2. Agree
3. Somewhat Agree
4. Disagree
5. Strongly Disagree

18) My women think that when I treat them with class and politeness that I really like them.

1. Strongly Agree
2. Agree
3. Somewhat Agree
4. Disagree
5. Strongly Disagree

19) When it comes to loving, I'm really afraid.

1. Strongly Agree
2. Agree
3. Somewhat Agree
4. Disagree
5. Strongly Disagree

20) My women don't realize that I am not interested in loving any woman.

1. Strongly Agree
2. Agree
3. Somewhat Agree
4. Disagree
5. Strongly Disagree

Below are the rating and scoring scales to determine if you are a Philophobic Player. If you are not, you can assess men who are. Enjoy the exercise.

Rating Scale
Strongly Agree = 5 points
Agree = 4 points
Somewhat Agree = 3 points
Disagree = 2 points
Strongly Disagree = 1 point

Chapter 7: The Philophobic Player

Scoring Scale
90-100 = You are definitely a Philophobic Player.
89-80 = You are a Philophobic Player.
79-70 = You may be a Philophobic Player.
69-60 = You are not a Philophobic Player.
59 and below = You are definitely not a Philophobic Player.

Women, it is your turn. You, also, may not have heard of this concept. Now that you know what it means, enjoy filling out the survey.

ARE YOU IN AN INTIMATE SEXUAL RELATIONSHIP WITH A PHILOPHOBIC PLAYER?

Directions: Answer the following questions honestly and find out if you are in an intimate sexual relationship with a Philophobic Player. Circle the number by the answer that best fits you.

1) I believe that my man is a gentleman.

1. Strongly Agree
2. Agree
3. Somewhat Agree
4. Disagree
5. Strongly Disagree

2) I believe that my man is a secure man.

1. Strongly Agree
2. Agree
3. Somewhat Agree
4. Disagree
5. Strongly Disagree

3) I believe that my man is a very confident man.

1. Strongly Agree
2. Agree
3. Somewhat Agree
4. Disagree
5. Strongly Disagree

4) My man acts as if he really loves me.

1. Strongly Agree
2. Agree
3. Somewhat Agree
4. Disagree
5. Strongly Disagree

5) My man doesn't want me to know that he has a fear of loving.

1. Strongly Agree
2. Agree
3. Somewhat Agree
4. Disagree
5. Strongly Disagree

6) My man doesn't want me to know that he has a fear of falling in love.

1. Strongly Agree
2. Agree
3. Somewhat Agree
4. Disagree
5. Strongly Disagree

7) My man doesn't want me to know that he has a fear of being in love.

1. Strongly Agree
2. Agree
3. Somewhat Agree
4. Disagree
5. Somewhat Disagree

8) My man doesn't want me to know that he has sexual relationships with two or more women at a time.

1. Strongly Agree
2. Agree
3. Somewhat Agree
4. Disagree
5. Strongly Disagree

9) My man doesn't want me to know that his major goal is to protect his feelings.

1. Strongly Agree
2. Agree
3. Somewhat Agree
4. Disagree
5. Strongly Disagree

10) My man doesn't want me to know that he is incapable of loving.

1. Strongly Agree
2. Agree
3. Somewhat Agree
4. Disagree
5. Strongly Disagree

11) My man doesn't want me to know that he really doesn't care about me.

1. Strongly Agree
2. Agree
3. Somewhat Agree
4. Disagree
5. Strongly Disagree

12) My man doesn't want me to know that he has no affection for me.

1. Strongly Agree
2. Agree

3. Somewhat Agree
4. Disagree
5. Strongly Disagree

13) My man doesn't want me to know that he has no fondness for me.

1. Strongly Agree
2. Agree
3. Somewhat Agree
4. Disagree
5. Strongly Disagree

14) My man doesn't want me to know that he is only concerned about himself.

1. Strongly Agree
2. Agree
3. Somewhat Agree
4. Disagree
5. Strongly Disagree

15) My man wants me to think that he really loves me.

1. Strongly Agree
2. Agree
3. Somewhat Agree
4. Disagree
5. Strongly Agree

16) My man wants me to think that the good sex I get from him is really showing me how much he loves me.

1. Strongly Agree
2. Agree
3. Somewhat Agree
4. Disagree
5. Strongly Disagree

17) My man wants me to believe that his knowing how to treat me is a good indicator of how much he loves me.

1. Strongly Agree
2. Agree
3. Somewhat Agree
4. Disagree
5. Somewhat Disagree

18) My man wants me to think that his treatment of me with class and politeness really shows me just how much he loves me.

1. Strongly Agree
2. Agree
3. Somewhat Agree
4. Disagree
5. Strongly Disagree

19) My man doesn't want me to know that when it comes to loving, he's really incapable of loving in an intimate sexual relationship.

1. Strongly Agree
2. Agree
3. Somewhat Disagree
4. Disagree
5. Strongly Disagree

20) My man doesn't want me to know that he's not interested in loving me or any other woman.

1. Strongly Agree
2. Agree
3. Somewhat Agree
4. Disagree
5. Strongly Disagree

Women, what did you think about the survey? To see if you are involved with a Philophobic Player, the rating and scoring scales will explain your connection or non-connection to this type of player.

Rating Scale
Strongly Agree = 5 points
Agree = 4 points
Somewhat Agree = 3 points
Disagree = 2 points
Strongly Disagree = 1 point

Scoring Scale
90-100 = You are definitely involved with a Philophobic Player.
89-80 = You are involved with a Philophobic Player.
79-70 = You may be involved with a Philophobic Player.
69-60 = You are not involved with a Philophobic Player.
59 and below = You are definitely not involved with a Philophobic Player.

Did you discover something about the man with whom you are involved? Did you
learn something about yourself? Let your truth lead you to a decision that will serve you well.

Chapter 8

The Down Low Player

I tell the females I'm heterosexual
But some males know I'm not
I dibble and dabble in all kinds of sex
More than games played on casino slots

I like it top
I like it bottom
I like it sideways too
I twist and turn
And bend and sway
With my sexual acrobatics
I capture my prey.

Women who like men
And men who like women
Are not off-limits to me
The homosexuals, bisexuals
And male and female transsexuals
Make up my sexual Long Island Ice Tea.

They call me low down
Cause I'm on the down low
And keep secrets about my sex life
My self-imposed gay order
Gives others hurt, pain and strife

Sexually wicked and sexually psychotic
Are just two of the labels
People give me
They think that I must be out of my mind
'Cause I'm bold and sexually free

Yes, I'm a trisexual
For better or worse
I have no guilt or remorse
I dare to try anything
With anybody
So come join me at my sexual resort.
I know I could contract an STD
Or someone could give me herpes for life
I still continue to have unprotected sex
Like a sex machine with a disease free device

Some say I have a death wish
Others say I'm Death Row bound
They claim that HIV/AIDS is beckoning for me
Calling me loudly without uttering a sound

Why should I care what anyone says
About the way I live my life
Even if I go straight to hell
The devil will give me sex
All day and all night.

Down Low—A Universal & Historical Happening

"Can you keep a secret?" "This ***must*** be kept secret." One is hard-pressed to find an individual who has not uttered the words in the above question and statement. At their base is any situation, behavior, event, or circumstance that individuals, organizations, or groups want concealed. From this point of view, the phrase "down low" has a broad meaning. The United States government labels confidential information as Top Secret and countries throughout the world pride themselves on maintaining a reticent position when it comes to matters of national security. Parents will tell their offspring to keep quiet about family matters to outsiders. Try finding a person who is without any knowledge that must be kept secret. It probably is an impossible task. Some type of "down low" behavior is exhibited by persons from all walks of life, irrespective of age, race, educational level, gender, and sexual orientation. It is demonstrated by persons of all walks of life. In this context, regardless of the demographics, persons from all four corners of the world have walked, are walking, and will walk on down low roads in their lives.

DL as an abbreviation for Down Low has been used to describe many different situations that vary dramatically. For example, DL in the baseball vernacular means that an injured player in Major League Baseball has been placed on the Disabled List. In football, DL means a Defensive Lineman. In education, DL represents Distance Learning. In the field of meteorology, DL means Day Light. And, in the banking industry, DL means a Direct Loan. The DLs discussed in this chapter are not remotely related to the meaning of any of these abbreviations.

Chapter 8: The Down Low Player

Down Low as discussed in this chapter is a concept that emerged in popular culture and received widespread attention in virtually every medium in mass media and the social network between 2001 and 2006. The origin of the history of this behavior is arguably traceable back to the beginning of human life. As presented here, it is rooted in the sexual behavior of married, single, and cohabitating males, who label themselves as heterosexual and publicly live heterosexual lives while engaging in sex with men, women, and sometimes, with persons of different sexual orientations, at the same time. It is not uncommon for some of these men to have children. Most of the men with whom they are sexually involved know about their sexual lifestyle but the women are kept in the dark. To fully understand this sexual behavior, an examination of the history of down low behavior and the major research conducted about it is warranted.

The Name Game

Much has been written in the past decade about males who have sex with males and females simultaneously. Yet, there are still questions surrounding this behavior, such as: Is there a history of this sexual behavior? What's in a label and do different labels about sexual behavior make a difference in how these males see themselves sexually and how they are seen by others? How did these males acquire this behavior? Who are they among the aggregate of all males? Is this a relatively new sexual behavioral pattern? Is one age group more likely to exhibit this behavior than others? Is there a higher probability of one ethnic/racial group engaging in this behavior than others? Do males of different socio-economic statuses, such as upper class, middle class, working class and non-working poor engage in this behavior? Do these males engage in this behavior with males who define themselves as heterosexual or are perceived as heterosexual as well as bisexuals, transsexuals, transgenders, female impersonators, homosexuals, or other labels of sexual orientations and sexual behaviors? Do some males have a preference to engage in sex with one or more of the groups mentioned? Does this down low sexual behavior evolve during the course of one's lifetime or does it exist from birth to death? If males exhibit this behavior in some part of their lives, does it mean that this behavior will definitely continue for the rest of their lives? The answers to these and other related questions are crucial to the understanding of males who have sex with males and females at the same time. A historical examination of the research on this sexual behavior will hopefully provide some answers to these queries.

Sigmund Freud, the father of psychoanalysis, is known for many theories on the sexuality of men and women. The penis envy complex, the Oedipus complex, and castration anxiety are probably some of the most noted theories associated with him. In addition to these aspects of the sexuality of males and females, Freud also wrote about bisexuality. Freud (as cited in Baumgardner, 2007) defined bisexuality as one having sexual desires and experiences with males and females. Baumgardner went on to point out that Freud studied bisexuality so much, he should be labeled "the doting mother of bisexuality" (Baumgardner, p. 43).

Although Freud wrote extensively about what he termed "innate bisexuality" (Baumgardner, p. 44), Wilhelm Fliess, a colleague and friend of Freud (as cited in Baumgardner) introduced his theory of biological bisexuality to Freud in 1898. Baumgardner asserts that Fliess and Freud believed that people are born bisexual. How much do you think Freud really knew about the causes of bisexuality? Let's examine his flip-flopping approach to the theoretical explanation of bisexuality. Freud claimed that as individuals go through psychological development and are affected by factors that are within and outside the self, most people become monosexual (having sex with persons of one sex only) while the bisexuality remains in a latent state. Freud later theorized that bisexuality was rooted in cultural and environmental factors. He stated that sexuality changes and evolves throughout one's life, thus concluding that as broad as the term "bisexuality" may be, it falls short of adequately describing all the drives for sex and love, and the physical connections humans feel toward some people at some point in time (Baumgardner). Let's examine Freud's theories on bisexuality and see if they shed any light on what is referred to in this chapter as Down Low Players.

At the time Freud wrote, Down Low as defined in this chapter was not in the lexicon. Freud wrote about bisexuality of males and females but he did not write about how bisexual men "played" or didn't "play" women and how and why they hide their total sexual experiences. Since Freud developed theories of bisexuality and did not conduct studies using bisexuals as subjects, his theories do not include social and cultural demographics of bisexuals. Freud did not use the concept of secrecy as a part of his analysis of bisexuality. One can surmise that since most of his theories emerged during the Victorian era, an era that promoted at least the appearance of strict, moral, religious, and social sexual norms, keeping the bisexual behavior "on the down low" for those who engaged in it, was a widespread practice. Keep these Freudian notions in mind when the discussion shifts to typologies of Down Low Players. See which theoretical perspective of Freud's they fit, if any.

Alfred Kinsey (as cited in Jones, 1997), a zoologist, biologist, and sexologist founded the Institute for Sex Research at Indiana University in 1947 where he was a professor. It was later renamed the Kinsey Institute because of the tremendous influence he had on the field of sexology in the 1940s and 1950s. Kinsey (as cited in

Baumgardner, 2007) was married with children and admitted to having sex with males during his marriage. He used the concept of polyamorous to label his sexual behavior. In the context in which he used it to explain his sexual behavior, it means having intimate sexual relationships with two or more males and females at the same time that goes beyond just recreational sex to include love. He was also bisexual. He did not claim to be secretive about his sexual relationships with men outside his marriage. In fact, he claimed that he and his wife agreed that both of them could have outside sexual relationships with other persons during their marriage.

Research conducted by Kinsey initially focused on bisexual behavior of men. According to Baumgardner (2007), Kinsey "found that a full 50 percent [of the men he studied] had had some bisexual experience" (p. 47). Taken from data collected by Kinsey in the 1940s and 1950s, the Kinsey Report (as cited in Reinisch, Beasley, Kent, & Kinsey Institute, 1990) noted, "Approximately one-third of all males are thought to have had at least one same-sex experience since puberty.... about 8 percent of U.S. males had had exclusively same-sex partners for at least a period of three years at some point in life" (pp.139-140). These data were taken from White middle-class subjects.

> [The data also indicated that] ...at least 25 percent of all American men have had a sexual experience with another male as teenagers or adults. (This is actually a conservative estimate—the data suggest that it is probably closer to one out of three American men.) Therefore, having had a same-sex experience is not unusual for men, even for those whose behavior is entirely heterosexual throughout the rest of their lives. (Reinisch, Beasley, Kent, & Kinsey Institute, 1990, p. 13)

In the foreword to *Sexual Behavior in the Human Male,* Sam Sloan (2010) states "that studies of vastly different ethnic/racial groups such as Chinese, Africans and Native American Indians have produced similar results to the results" of Kinsey's studies in 1948. He asserts that these results suggest "that all humans, regardless of cultural groupings, have about the same sexual habits" (Sloan, 2010).

Kinsey (1948) developed his well-known Kinsey Scale to describe sexual orientations which rates three elements of sexuality: 1) sexual desires, 2) sexual practices, and 3) sexual identity. This breakdown was determined from data he received from the responses to 350 questions that inquired about the sexual histories of his students. More than 5,300 males were said to be interviewed. These were face-to-face interviews as opposed to questionnaires. The scale had six categories that ranged from 0-6. Zero represented exclusively heterosexual. Number 1 represented predominantly heterosexual behavior (only incidental homosexual experiences); number 2 was predominantly heterosexual behavior, but more than incidental homosexual relationships. The third range was equally heterosexual, homosexual, and bisexual. Number 4 was predominantly homosexual but more than incidental heterosexual behavior. Five was predominantly homosexual with only incidental heterosexual encounters and category 6 was exclusively homosexual. Kinsey discovered that heterosexual and homosexual labels of men's sexual behavior did not explain the degrees to which they practice sex with women and men. Kinsey brought to light the sexual variations that existed among men in their sexual experiences with men and women during their lifetime. As a result of these and other breakthrough findings on men's sexual behavior, Kinsey was and still is viewed as the leading sexologist of his time and beyond among many scientists.

Humphreys (1970), a sociologist, conducted a study on married and unmarried men who labeled themselves and lived public lives as heterosexual, while at the same time meeting at public places, such as public restrooms, parks, and truck stops to engage in impersonal sex acts with other men. He pointed out that secrecy, keeping it on the down low, was the major guiding force in the selection of the public places where these sex acts took place. Humphreys oftentimes served as the lookout person, or in tearoom language, the "watchqueen" at these impersonal meeting places. The men did not know that he was conducting a study for his PhD dissertation. He would then go to their homes under the guise of collecting data for a grant that had nothing to do with tearoom behavior of men who engaged in sex with men and women. The men had no idea that the same man who served as their lookout person in the impersonal places where they had sexual encounters with males was collecting additional data about them that had virtually nothing to do with their tearoom behavior and was welcomed in their homes to do so. As Humphreys points out in different parts of his book, the men at their abode were totally different from the behavior they presented in the "tearooms".

To get a better sense of the similarities of these men in their home life experiences, he divided the men who meet at these places into four types. Type I was referred to as Trade. He stated that these males earned that name from the gay subculture. The men in this category have been married, one was separated and another divorced. Their occupations ranged from a member of the armed forces to a carpenter to a minister at a Pentecostal church. Five in six were White. Of the 19 subjects in this category, 14 had completed high school, three had completed college and five had had less than 12 years of school. They had children, as many as seven. They were well-respected in their neighborhoods and they were viewed by others as good husbands and fathers. Humphreys believed that a preoccupation with their image influenced their decision to use a method of sexuality with men that was quick, inexpensive, and impersonal.

Type II was labeled The Ambisexual. In this context, the label was describing men who visited tearooms and had a sexual orientation and attraction to persons of either sex. Humphreys highlights a businessman who was married and had tearoom sex with men with whom he had established a business relationship as well as men he did not know. The man's out-of-state business meetings allowed him to extend his ambisexual ways. He was married into a distinguished family, had attended a prestigious college, and enjoyed an upper middle-class lifestyle. He had his first sexual experience with a male when he was nine or ten at a summer camp. He later married the female he impregnated and was still married 18 years later. He admitted to having sex with his wife three-four times a week and visited the tearooms every day. He made the distinction between sex with men in the tearooms and sex with his wife by rationalizing that sex in the tearooms is really not sex. "Sex is something I have with my wife in bed. It's not as if I were committing adultery by getting my rocks off, or going down on some guy in a tearoom. I get a kick out of it." This is how he expresses his great devotion to his wife and children: "They're my life." At no point did he consider his wife while he was involved in tearoom sexual relationships. All evidence indicated that as father, citizen, businessman, and church member, his behavior as viewed by his peers has been exemplary.

Type III, The Gay, is defined as the most truly "gay" of all participant types. The age range was from 19 to 50. One of this type that Humphreys highlighted was a 24-year-old college student whose older male lover financially supported him. His mannerisms and gestures may be viewed as effeminate. They met in the park. He lived a gay life at night and at day. A response that typified males in this group was, "I prefer men but I would make a good wife for the right man."

Type IV, The Closet Queens, is a slang term in homosexual communities. They keep their gay relationships hidden, whether they are married or single. Some of their characteristics as cited by Humphreys are: 1.They have few friends, only a minority of whom are involved in tearoom activity, 2. Half of them are Roman Catholic in religion, 3. They work as teachers, postmen, salesmen and clerks, usually for large corporations. 4. Most of them have completed only high school, although there were a few exceptionally well-educated in this group, and 5. The overwhelming majority is White.

It should be noted that at the time of this study (as cited in Elkins & King, 1996), Humphreys was married with children. It was later revealed that he and his wife divorced after two decades of marriage and he started living an openly gay life. His study remains a landmark study in the area of married and single men who publicly present a heterosexual identity to the public and engage in clandestine, down low relationships with other men.

The Down Low (DL) Media Explosion

In 1995, the sultry sound of Brian McKnight laid out lyrics about a man "On the Down Low" who was involved with a woman who was married or living with a man but did not want anyone to know about it. In that same year, R. Kelly released the song "Down Low (Nobody Has to Know)," featuring the Isley Brothers. These lyrics told a story about a single man involved in a relationship with another man's woman who was possibly married. He was telling her in the song to keep it on the down low because nobody has to know. Ron Isley, who plays the role of the other man, sings, "...how can you go so low," apparently to the woman. These two songs gave a broad meaning to being "on the down low" that included heterosexual relationships with single and possibly persons. However, the majority of the literary coverage of persons on the down low focused on men who labeled themselves as "straight" and were perceived by others as heterosexual while at the same time engaging in sexual acts with males. "Straight" is used synonymously with heterosexuality.

From 2001 to 2006, a plethora of articles in newspapers and magazines, and several books were written about the down low men as defined in this chapter. In 2001, *Los Angeles Times, USA Today, Chicago Sun-Times, San Francisco Chronicle,* and *Village Voice,* just to name a few reported on the down low phenomenon among males claiming to be heterosexual at the same time they were involved sexually with males. In 2003, the *New York Times* and *Detroit Free Press* continued this coverage of down low men. A reporter from the *Detroit Free Press* interviewed E. Lynn Harris, an openly gay male, regarding this down low sexual behavior. His position was that men who engage in this behavior are not just on the down low, they are ***low down*** men on the down low. He based this on the health risks to which they subjected women with whom they are involved and the deception that guides and frames this behavior. The following year, *Essence* magazine commissioned him to meet with some down low males at his residence. Prior to this meeting (published in an article in the July, 2004 issue of *Essence*), Harris had stated that he could tell a down low man from a truly heterosexual male. When four of the six men who were on the down low arrived at his condominium, he changed his tune. He then confessed that he could not tell that some of these men were on the down low.

King (2004) arguably received the most notoriety and media exposure from his book on down low behavior among Black males. He revealed in graphic language the sexual experiences these men have with men and women and their failure to disclose their down low homosexual behavior to the women with whom they were involved.

King also noted that some of the greatest dangers in these relationships have resulted in an increase in HIV/AIDS victims among Black females. He gives very timely advice to women to aid them in protecting themselves against the sexual behavior of down low men and any men who have a high propensity to place women's physical and emotional health at risk. The following highlight his advice: 1) don't be too desperate to have a man, 2) ask questions about the man's sexual history and sexual practices, 3) investigate men, and 4) make them use a condom. King described some of his down low sexual behavior in this book. However, when King first appeared in April, 2004 on the *Oprah Winfrey Show,* he completely denied his homosexuality. In a subsequent appearance in 2010, he did admit to his homosexual behavior. In fact, he changed his label of himself from a "straight" man on the down low to a gay man.

Boykin (2005) wrote a book that received media attention as well. It emphasized the notion that males from ethnic and racial groups other than African Americans participated in down low homosexual acts while claiming to be 100% heterosexual. His point buttresses the studies quoted above. In the same year, a dramatic movie about the sexual and romantic relationship between two men received national acclaim. They too were on the down low as defined by this chapter. The movie *Brokeback Mountain* that opened in theaters in 2005 illustrated how these men went back and forth between their homosexual and heterosexual relationships. They failed to notify those who knew them only as heterosexual of their homosexual/bisexual/ down low behavior. This movie depicted how males can fool others, especially women, about their true sexuality and how they practice their true sexuality.

Although the media attention to the down low phenomenon has decreased dramatically, the behavior continues. Unknowing women still fall victim to this behavior. Many of these men are so adept at the cover-up of their true sexuality, family members, friends, coworkers and associates, more often than not, are clueless about who they really are sexually. With all of this media exposure, do you think you can recognize down low (DL) males? The next section will test your awareness of this sexual issue.

How's Your "Gaydar" Detector?

A group of female students left a marriage and family class after a discussion about male-female relationships and went to their dormitory to continue the discussion. They decided to write about their greatest fears when selecting a mate for marriage. They later revealed to me that their number one fear was dating and marrying a man who they thought was heterosexual but discovered he was bisexual, down low homosexual, or some other form of sexuality that falls outside of heterosexuality in label and in practice. Their hope was that their "gaydar" would provide them with signs and signals that would allow them to identify non-heterosexual men and therefore avoid intimate contact with them. These symbols of non-heterosexual behavior will be determined by the women's intuition when making decisions about down low males based on mannerisms, gestures, and facial expressions that are more associated with male gay behavior.

"Gaydar" is a word that some say was first used on the national television program *Saturday Night Live*. Others say it was first used on the national television series, *Sex in the City*; still others said that while they use the word, they don't know its origin. It is known that a website called "gaydar" was established in 1999 in South Africa. However, this is a dating website that serves as a social medium connection for gays, bisexuals, and homosexual women and men. Therefore, this use of gaydar is not the focus of this section or this chapter. Gaydar will be used in this chapter only to get at the extent to which women think that they can recognize a male who presents himself as heterosexual when in fact he is bisexual/homosexual or some other sexual orientation.

The operative question to women is: Can you tell? E. Lynn Harris thought he could tell the down low males from other males but he couldn't. If he couldn't, do you think you can? To get a better sense of the difficulty of gay and down low males in recognizing down low men, they were asked if they could identify them and if so, what mannerisms, gestures, and facial expressions did they consider in their decision. First, they talked about why down low males put the time, energy, and effort into their disguises to keep their down low behavior a secret. One male stated, "Some of them go to extremes to keep their sexuality a secret because they're living a double life and they are afraid that if it comes out, it will ruin their image." Another male said, "Some of them have children and they know that if their baby mamas found out they were on the DL, they would snatch their parental rights from them." Still another commented that some of them live with women and go out to gay bars to be with men. "They don't want the woman to find out so they get a male sexual partner who is not in the same area or community where they live."

It was also noted by a gay male that some DL men go out of state and out of the country to get their down low homosexual acts on. "They will travel to Thailand, the Caribbean, Brazil and other places that are known to have free love-free sex. Even though these places are seen as places where females go to get their free love and free sex on, down low men can satisfy their sexual desires with just as much ease at these places." When it comes to going to church and participating in church activities, many down low men view this as another reason to stay on the down low. One interviewee noted, "Some of the DL men are too scared to come out because they are in the church. They know that some people may suspect that they are DL but they don't know it. If they knew it, they may not respect you like they used to and they will act differently toward you. That's why a lot of DL men try to play that super-masculine role in public." Another interviewee pointed out that some DL males try hard to hide it because "they are ashamed." He went on to say, "I wish I had not ever come out because people treat you differently, including your family. As long as they are curious about it, they will give you the benefit of the doubt. You get more respect when they are curious about your sexuality. Society treats you differently but not everybody. Some people try to be more liberal and say who cares—some people are scared to have you around them and their children. Some of them really think that you will sexually molest their children. And in the church, some people are afraid to have you in the nursery 'cause they think you gonna do something to their children. My oldest sister had a hard time with it (his gay sexuality) for 10-15 years. She told me she had a problem with it because I'm her only brother. A therapist talked to her, her cousin and some other persons. She's fine with it now. She started to accept it in the mid-1990s. She will meet my gay friends and play cards with them and have a good time. When she saw that I wasn't flamboyant and I'm on the DL and when she saw women hollering at me and hitting on me, she became more accepting."

From these males' points of view, a major factor in males remaining on the down low is preventing others, especially family, friends, girlfriends, coworkers, and others who fall in the category of significant others from knowing their true sexuality. One gay male stated that he could spot a DL male 50% of the time. He went on to say the problem with women recognizing DL males has a lot to do with how DL males relate to their male partners. For example, "the 20- to 30-year-olds may introduce their male partner to a heterosexual as, 'this is my boy' or 'this is my cousin' or 'this is my homeboy.' The DLs in their '40s and '50s may say, 'this is my nephew' or 'this is my son' or 'this is my coworker.' I was my first lover's 'brother'. He would say this to his baby mama and to his new girlfriend. Sometimes he would say that I was his high school classmate."

Another male stated, "It's too hard to really just tell because the DLs try too hard to protect themselves. But the best advice I can give women is to observe their eyes. The eyes will tell the story. See if he looks at certain guys. You can tell a lot about the guys if you pay attention to their eyes. Sometimes women can tell by the kind of sex they want. Say for example if they want sex that's more like the kind of sex gay men have, that may also be a sign but not necessarily 'cause some heterosexual males just like some sex that's more associated with gay sex." He also stated that a lot of women who are sexually involved with a DL man may suspect it but they don't want to believe it. "I have told a female friend of mine that her man was on the DL. She asked me how did I know and I told her that he had hit on me. She really didn't want to believe me then. She even stopped speaking to me. The only thing that convinced her was when she came home early from school and caught him and his lover in a sex act. He almost talked himself out of that because he told her that he had never done it before and that he was just doing it because the guy told him he would give him $200 and since they needed money to pay the rent, he did it."

It appears that it is virtually improbable for women to know for a fact if a male is on the DL unless they witness them in a homosexual sex act. Some DL males are more muscular and manly in mannerisms, gestures, and facial expressions than some 100% heterosexual males. A helpful hint to women may be to ask other males, straight or gay, who care about you and have your best interests at heart, about the male in your life and be inclined to accept their assessment of him. It doesn't mean that they can tell you for a fact if the male in your life is gay, bisexual, or of some other sexual orientation label. What they can do is help you to observe certain behaviors that may lead you to make a more informed decision.

Below are some typologies of down low players. Do you think you would identify them as Down Low players?

Mr. Straight by Day and Gay by Night (aka Mr. SDGN)

Mr. SDGN plays the role of this heterosexual player during the daylight hours. He brags about having two or three women at the same time that he is involved with one-three males. Here is his explanation: "There are some fine women out here and there are some fine men. I like 'em both. They all give me something that I need. The women arc like all-purpose women. They cook, satisfy you sexually, give you money and buy you things, wash your clothes and iron your clothes. All you have to do is make sure you make them happy in the bed. When one can't give me what I want, I just call one of the other ones." The same male meets his gay friends at the gay bar where he works. He is quick to point out that he is not the only down low guy who works at the gay bars. "Males like me can pick and choose who they want without people who know them during their daytime straight life ever becoming suspicious."

He notes, "When you work at a gay bar as a bouncer or security guard, your straight friends believe you when you tell them that the club can't afford to hire a gay guy as a bouncer or a security guard because nobody would take him seriously. They believe me and I continue my double lifestyle." He also talked about some down low males who are bartenders, cooks, and waiters. Some also own their clubs. "They make their sexual connections where they work and their daytime friends don't have a clue about their night life. This is the best way to combine business with pleasure."

Women, do you think you could identify Mr. Straight by Day and Gay by Night? If you hired a private investigator, that person may be able to gather enough evidence to convince you. Otherwise, you may remain in the dark.

Chapter 8: The Down Low Player

Tom the Trisexual

Tom the Trisexual does not care if the persons with whom he becomes sexually involved are female, gay, transsexual, transgender, bisexual, or any type of sexual orientation. He loves sex with different persons, of different sexual backgrounds, and he loves different sexual positions. A DL player who is the prototype of Tom the Trisexual explained it this way: "When you have sex with a lot of different people with slightly different sexual desires, they introduce you to so much more and they are more versatile and they like you to be more versatile. Sometimes I like a more feminine acting lover and sometimes I want a more masculine lover. Sometimes I like to take the top role (the penetrating role), and sometimes I want the bottom. I like it top and bottom. (The top and bottom positions are sexual positions that are well-known by this language in the gay and DL communities.) I also like a straight-up woman sometimes. I guess I'm just greedy. I shuffle, I deal, and I flip-flop." The last sentence is just another way for him to say that he plays the role of the man, the woman, and sometimes he switches from one role to another during a sexual encounter. The way he describes the frequency of his sexual encounters and the impersonal way in which some of them manifest, it appears that he may have a death wish. He acts like he wants to die but doesn't have whatever it takes to pull the trigger on the gun. As a substitute, he participates in unprotected sex virtually every time he performs a sex act or engages in different sexual encounters. He alleges the few times that he did use protection, it was only because his partner threatened to not have sex with him. By the way, females, when I asked Tom if he were interested in changing his sexual lifestyle, he said, "Absolutely not. I'm having too much fun."

Peter the Prostitute

"It seems like everything is about money, about dollars and cents when it comes to the DL men." The male saying this felt that he was exploited financially by his male lover. He claims that DL men can get money from the guy and from the woman. He said, in reference to his lover, "He will throw me under the bus if a woman comes along that likes him and gives him money. See, a lot of them (DL men), go to women who's laying out more money and doing more for him. For instance, my lover asked me to pay his phone bill and when I didn't, he went to his woman and she paid it. He leaves me and goes to her when she does more for him than I do. One day I'm going to get tired of this and leave him alone." This is a gay male who knows he's in a relationship with a DL male who is also involved with at least one female. He knows about the woman but the woman does not know about him. Therefore, she's in a more vulnerable position than he is.

Peter the Prostitute stated that he started this sexual lifestyle at the age of 21 because he had lost his job and he needed money. In addition to prostitution as a way to get money, he was also a clip artist. That is, he would rob the men who solicited him. During this time, he had a girlfriend who, as he noted, didn't have a clue about his prostitution and stealing from the males who solicited him. "I made big money and what I didn't get for the service I performed, I stole from them. One time while I was having sex with this man, I clipped him for five grand. I waited until I had him in the heat of the moment, then I clipped him. When it was over, I ran like hell to get away from him before he knew that I had clipped him." Peter also cited a situation in which the john pulled a gun on him and they fought over the gun. "I ran for my life. I was scared but I had to get over my fear because a scared 'hoe don't make no money." In spite of this encounter, Peter viewed male prostitution as easy "most of the times, because they pay me to let them perform sex acts on me. Most of the time, I didn't have to do nothing for them. That's easy money." Peter has continued this behavior. His girlfriend, as far as he knows, is without knowledge of his life as a male prostitute and a clip artist.

Larry the Live-in Boyfriend

When it comes to women, Larry is a serial live-in mate. That is, he moves from one woman's house, to another woman's house, and on and on. He stated that he knows he will eventually get put out because he really doesn't contribute to the finances of the house and other households needs. "I keep them satisfied sexually. That's my role." While he is in and out of these women's lives, he's having sexual encounters with men. When asked how he managed to keep those two lives separate and keep the women from knowing, he said it is simple. "First, I let the women know that I don't like to go out with women because I like to do manly things when I go out, like go to football games, basketball games, baseball games, shoot pool, and play cards. Since she is not interested in doing these things, I'm home free. Even if she was interested, I wouldn't let her go with me. My men know that I have a woman and that's okay with them as long as they can see me most of the time when they want to." What is interesting about this type of DL male is that most of them are with females who have children by them. Not only are the women kept in the dark, the children are also.

These Down Low Player typologies in no way exhaust all the different types of DL males. They do provide enough variety of what women can expect in these undercover, double-dealing relationships. Remember women, paying attention to your mate's lifestyles and activities within the home and away from home may be matters of life and death. Men, look at your risks as well. Are the sexual encounters worth your health and possibly your life?

Below is a survey for the males to determine if they fall in the Down Low Player category.

ARE YOU A DOWN LOW PLAYER?

Directions: Answer the following questions honestly and find out if you are a Down Low Player. Circle the number by the answer that best fits you.

1) I like having sex with women and homosexuals.
1. Strongly Agree
2. Agree
3. Somewhat Agree
4. Disagree
5. Strongly Disagree

2) I like having sex with women and bisexuals.
1. Strongly Agree
2. Agree
3. Somewhat Agree
4. Disagree
5. Strongly Disagree

3) I like having sex with heterosexuals and transsexuals.
1. Strongly Agree
2. Agree
3. Somewhat Agree
4. Disagree
5. Strongly Disagree

4) I prefer to have sex with men.
1. Strongly Agree
2. Agree
3. Somewhat Agree
4. Disagree
5. Strongly Disagree

5) I like hanging around gay bars.
1. Strongly Agree
2. Agree
3. Somewhat Agree
4. Disagree
5. Strongly Disagree

6) I like looking at porn movies that show men having sex with men.
1. Strongly Agree
2. Agree

3. Somewhat Agree
4. Disagree
5. Strongly Disagree

7) My male friends come first in my life, even before the woman I'm having sex with.

1. Strongly Agree
2. Agree
3. Somewhat Agree
4. Disagree
5. Strongly Disagree

8) I don't tell women that I have sex with people who are not females or were not born females.

1. Strongly Agree
2. Agree
3. Somewhat Agree
4. Disagree
5. Strongly Disagree

9) I don't let the thought of getting a venereal disease or herpes or HIV/AIDS stop me from my sexual experiences with males and females and others of different sexual orientations.

1. Strongly Agree
2. Agree
3. Somewhat Agree
4. Disagree
5. Strongly Disagree

10) I like having sex with persons from different sexual walks of life.

1. Strongly Agree
2. Agree
3. Somewhat Agree
4. Disagree
5. Strongly Disagree

11) I will try almost anything that will give me sexual pleasure with anybody.

1. Strongly Agree
2. Agree
3. Somewhat Agree
4. Disagree
5. Strongly Disagree

12) I deceive heterosexual women about my sexual behavior.

1. Strongly Agree
2. Agree
3. Somewhat Agree
4. Disagree
5. Strongly Disagree

13) I can't have a monogamous relationship.
1. Strongly Agree
2. Agree
3. Somewhat Agree
4. Disagree
5. Strongly Disagree

14) I control my own sexual destiny.

1. Strongly Agree
2. Agree
3. Somewhat Agree
4. Disagree
5. Strongly Disagree

15) I'm not concerned about who I hurt as a result of my sexual appetite and my sexual behavior.
1. Strongly Agree
2. Agree
3. Somewhat Agree
4. Disagree
5. Strongly Disagree

16) I don't see anything wrong with being bisexual.
1. Strongly Agree
2. Agree
3. Somewhat Agree
4. Disagree
5. Strongly Disagree

17) I don't use a condom and other devices all the time.
1. Strongly Agree
2. Agree
3. Somewhat Agree
4. Disagree
5. Strongly Disagree

18) I believe that sexual variety is the spice of life.
1. Strongly Agree
2. Agree
3. Somewhat Agree
4. Disagree
5. Strongly Disagree

19) I think about getting a sexually transmitted disease but those thoughts don't stop my desire to have a lot of different types of unprotected sex.
1. Strongly Agree
2. Agree
3. Somewhat Agree
4. Disagree
5. Strongly Disagree

20) I like the way men make me feel; I like how women make me feel; I like how homosexuals and others make me feel; I like it all.

1. Strongly Agree
2. Agree
3. Somewhat Agree
4. Disagree
5. Strongly Disagree

Use this breakdown to assign points and tally them.

Rating Scale
Strongly Agree = 5 points
Agree = 4 points
Somewhat Agree = 3 points
Disagree = 2 points
Strongly Disagree = 1 point

The scale below will allow you to take your total score and see where it falls in the categories below.

Scoring Scale
90-100 = You are definitely a Down Low Player.
89-80 = You are a Down Low Player.
79-70 = You may be a Down Low Player.
69-60 = You are not a Down Low Player.
59 and below = You are definitely not a Down Low Player.

Did you discover anything about yourself that you didn't know? If so, what do you plan to do about it?

Females, below is your survey. See if you discover something about yourself that you didn't know.

ARE YOU IN A RELATIONSHIP WITH A DOWN LOW PLAYER?

Directions: Answer the following questions honestly and find out if you are in an intimate sexual relationship with a Down Low Player. Circle the number by the answer that best fits you.

1) My man hangs around with too many men.

1. Strongly Agree
2. Agree
3. Somewhat Agree
4. Disagree
5. Strongly Disagree

2) My man associates with males who act like they are gay. They have a lot of stereotypical mannerisms.

1. Strongly Agree
2. Agree
3. Somewhat Agree
4. Disagree
5. Strongly Disagree

3) My man acts like he forgets that I have a vagina when we make love.

1. Strongly Agree
2. Agree
3. Somewhat Agree
4. Disagree
5. Strongly Disagree

4) My man sees nothing wrong with going to clubs that have transvestites/drag queens.

1. Strongly Agree
2. Agree
3. Somewhat Agree
4. Disagree
5. Strongly Disagree

5) Every time my man and I see a young fine man, he looks at him harder and longer than I do.

1. Strongly Agree
2. Agree
3. Somewhat Agree
4. Disagree
5. Strongly Disagree

6) My man is always talking about his male friends and what they are doing in their lives.

1. Strongly Agree
2. Agree
3. Somewhat Agree
4. Disagree
5. Strongly Disagree

7) My man compares me to his male friends and tells me all the things that they do better than I do, like cooking and cleaning.

1. Strongly Agree
2. Agree
3. Somewhat Agree
4. Disagree
5. Strongly Disagree

8) My man is always coming home with male friends; he says they are his high school classmates, or his college roommates, or his coworkers.

1. Strongly Agree

2. Agree
3. Somewhat Agree
4. Disagree
5. Strongly Disagree

9) My man never uses a condom.

1. Strongly Agree
2. Agree
3. Somewhat Agree
4. Disagree
5. Strongly Disagree

10) My man never wants me to go to the clubs and bars where he goes.

1. Strongly Agree
2. Agree
3. Somewhat Agree
4. Disagree
5. Strongly Disagree

11) My man likes to look at porn movies that have men having sex with men.

1. Strongly Agree
2. Agree
3. Somewhat Agree
4. Disagree
5. Strongly Disagree

12) My man has too many men texting him all the time.

1. Strongly Agree
2. Agree
3. Somewhat Agree
4. Disagree
5. Strongly Disagree

13) My man will change our plans to be with his male friends.

1. Strongly Agree
2. Agree
3. Somewhat Agree
4. Disagree
5. Strongly Disagree

14) My man acts like he cares more about his male friends than he cares about me.

1. Strongly Agree
2. Agree
3. Somewhat Agree
4. Disagree
5. Strongly Disagree

15) My man dresses up like a woman sometimes when we are home alone.

1. Strongly Agree

2. Agree
3. Somewhat Agree
4. Disagree
5. Strongly Disagree

16) My man sometimes acts too feminine for me.

1. Strongly Agree
2. Agree
3. Somewhat Agree
4. Disagree
5. Strongly Disagree

17) My man comes home sometimes smelling like men's cologne that he doesn't use.

1. Strongly Agree
2. Agree
3. Somewhat Agree
4. Disagree
5. Strongly Disagree

18) Sometimes when my man and I have sex, my man wants me to call him the B word and take on a masculine role.

1. Strongly Agree
2. Agree
3. Somewhat Agree
4. Disagree
5. Strongly Disagree

19) My man believes that there's nothing wrong with being a transsexual.

1. Strongly Agree
2. Agree
3. Somewhat Agree
4. Disagree
5. Strongly Agree

20) My man sometimes acts like he can't stand homosexuals.

1. Strongly Agree
2. Agree
3. Somewhat Agree
4. Disagree
5. Strongly Disagree

Below is the rating scale to determine the extent to which you are or are not a woman involved with a DL Player.

Rating Scale
Strongly Agree = 5 points
Agree = 4 points

Somewhat Agree = 3 points
Disagree = 2 points
Strongly Disagree = 1 point

Add your scores and see where you fall in the scoring scale below.

Scoring Scale
90-100 = You are definitely involved with a Down Low Player.
89-80 = You are involved with a Down Low Player.
79-70 = You may be involved with a Down Low Player.
69-60 = You are not involved with a Down Low Player.
59 and below = You are definitely not involved with a Down Low Player.

Have you come upon any revelations about yourself? Are they good or bad? If they are not positive, do you plan to do anything about them? The verdict is yours!

Part III

Lessons Learned

Intimate sexual relationships in the 21st century are an area of study that has received widespread attention. The world of players in male-female relationships is no exception to this growing phenomenon. This book has presented some startling revelations about men who define themselves as players. In their own words, they describe how they misuse, mistreat, abandon, neglect, and abuse women. There are passages with testimonies of women attesting to the type of ill-fated treatment they receive from these men. In case after case, players discuss and sometimes brag about women they "play" in relationships. This book is meant to serve as a guide to healthier and more wholesome relationships for women who are seeking committed relationships. It is hoped that now that players have read this book, they will reexamine their behavior in male-female relationships and their treatment of the women with whom they are involved. If the lessons are learned that appeared throughout this book and those that are summarized below, men and women, players and non-players will benefit from them and grow into a higher level of understanding of what it means to have a joyous, peaceful, prosperous, and loving relationship and what it takes for these type of relationships to develop and sustain themselves over time.

Lessons Women Need to Learn About the Games These Players Play

The lessons women need to learn about men who define themselves as players and act this behavior out in relationships did not originate with this book. They are lessons that women needed to learn decades ago. The two player groups discussed in this book are delineated here to distinguish between the behavior of each and what women need to learn who engage in intimate sexual relationships with them. The Truth Tellers openly admit to their player status in male-female relationships and The Betrayers are hell-bent on ***not*** revealing who they really are. The most salient lesson women must learn is that their sexual behavior largely determines the sexual behavior of men. The more women tolerate from men, the more men will ask them or tell them to tolerate. Therefore, if women are disenchanted with the large number of "ineligible" eligible bachelors who refer to themselves as players, they may benefit from a change in their own behavior and the type of intimate sexual relationships in which they involve themselves. Below are lessons women need to learn about men who see themselves as players and wave their player card as if it is their badge of honor.

Players who fall in the category of The Truth Tellers have these lessons for women to learn.

- Women cannot change men. If men change, they decide when they change, how they change, and how long the change will continue.
- Game playing is a way of life for players.
- Whenever men appear to be "too good to be true", not only are they probably too good to be true in actuality, women need to ask, "What are their motives?"
- Barring physical force and rape, men cannot do anything to women unless they allow them.
- Players will get what they want from women without feeling guilt or remorse if women let them.
- Players will do as little as possible for women.
- Players will tell women what women want to hear.
- Mothers are the first ones who may influence the development of a male into a player.
- Players will be players as long as women tolerate their player behavior.
- Players are not interested in commitment or marriage.
- Players are not interested in being in love.
- Players enjoy being players.
- Players want what they want, when they want it.
- Players come in many types, from the highly educated, wealthy, gainfully employed, cultivated, and highly intelligent to the barely educated, economically poor, unemployed, homeless, incarcerated, and lacking in social graces.
- Some players are very selective about the women they choose and others will almost accept any woman.
- Players intentionally have two or more women so that they will have a better chance of controlling their emotions.
- Players will continue to be players until they decide to hang up their players' shoes.

The lessons learned in this section are for the mothers of Mama's Boy Players. They can also benefit mothers and fathers of players who fall in the other categories.

- Teach your son that how he treats others may be just as important as loving and liking himself and how he treats himself.
- Rear and socialize your son in such a way that if you were not his mother and if you were in his age range, you would be honored and privileged to be his wife.
- Nurture and teach your sons how to be responsible in male-female relationships.

- Teach your son to strive to develop a King-Queen relationship with the female with whom he is involved. It will benefit both of them.
- Teach your son how to respect and honor the female with whom he is in an intimate-sexual relationship.
- Teach your son to develop a combination of an interdependent and an independent relationship with his mate. An interdependent relationship will be guided by the philosophy and behavior of: I teach you, you teach me; I learn from you and you learn from me. An independent relationship with your mate means that you have the abilities and knowledge to lead, make sound decisions, protect, and provide.
- Teach your son to place a high premium on his mate's character. Value a mate's character that is composed of dignity, integrity, principles, morals, and positive values.
- Teach your son to treat his mate the way a man who loves, respects, and values his mother, grandmother, daughter, sister, and other significant females should treat them.
- Teach your son the importance of developing a friendship relationship ***first*** with his mate, before the development of a sexual relationship.
- Teach your son that in relationships of significance, sacrifices are made to keep the relationship moving forward. Teach him that selfless acts in relationships don't reduce his adulthood and manhood, they enhance them.
- Teach your son that an "I must win mentality" may not be the best and most useful mentality in intimate-sexual relationships. Sometimes, it is not about who won or who was right, it's about what's best for the maintenance and sustainability of a meaningful, healthy, prosperous, and wholesome relationship.
- Teach your son the art, skill, and beauty in treating women like ladies, including you, his mother, his mate, his grandmother, daughter, sister, and other females.
- Teach your son to value females, even when they act like they don't value themselves.

Players who conceal their player behavior have these lessons for women to learn.

- Deceit is practiced on women as an art and a skill.
- These players cannot be trusted.
- These players will betray you.
- These players are afraid to love and women cannot change this.
- Some of these players are preoccupied with their need to maintain power and control over their emotions.
- Some of these players have a strong need to have or think they have power, control, and domination over the women with whom they are involved.
- Lying is a way of life for these players.

- These players are so good at their deception, the likelihood is that they will fool the most educated women in fields that study social behavior in general and men's behavior in particular.
- These players can fool the most street-smart women.

The following statements are summarized suggestions that may serve as valuable lessons for women to learn. Listen to what other men say about men's behavior in male-female relationships. Make sure those men in whom you confide genuinely love you and have your best interests at heart. Some fathers, brothers, sons, uncles, and male friends may be prime candidates for this important role. Take your time when getting involved with a man. Use the time you take to determine if his words are consistent with his behavior and if his behavior is consistent over time. Admit any harsh realities that you may discover in the behavior of players. Remember, as a woman, you don't understand men as much as you think you do, or as much as you should or as much as you need to. Also, don't forget that women cannot change men; only a man changes himself. If women want a man with integrity, morals, dignity, and genuine love for women, they must refrain from accepting behavior that does not resemble these qualities.

All players who fit in the categories of The Truth Tellers and The Betrayers can benefit from these lessons to learn

- Whenever women appear to be "too good to be true", not only are they probably too good to be true in actuality, men need to ask, "What are their motives?"
- Women who feel betrayed or deceived may resort to deceptive tactics of their own to get back at the betrayers and deceivers.
- Women who do everything for you are the most dangerous. They have a goal. Their goal is to get men in a position of dependency on them and have them think that they can't live without them.
- Remember, "hell has no fury like a woman scorned." Beware of a woman who believes she was scorned.
- Violence in domestic relationships is on the rise among women. Players may be the receivers of some of this violence if women feel misused, emotionally abused, and mistreated.
- If players value inner peace and a sense of freedom, these values may be compromised by being a player.

Players, don't ever forget this: ***You can play games for so long and you will eventually run out of games to play and women with whom to play them.*** For those men who are determined to continue their game playing ways long after they are without any workable games to play may qualify to be the poster men for the phrase, ***"There's no fool like an old fool".***

References

Barlow, D. H. (1988). *Anxiety and Its Disorders: The Nature and Treatment of Anxiety and Panic*. New York: Guilford Press.

Baumgardner, J. (2007). *Look Both Ways: Bisexual Politics*. New York: Farrar, Straus and Giroux.

Boykin, K. (2005). *Beyond the Down Low: Sex, Lies, and Denial in Black America*. New York: Carroll & Graf.

Cooley, C. H. (1902). *Human Nature and the Social Order.* New York: Scribner.

Diagnostic and Statistical Manual of Mental Disorders (DSM IV-TR). (2000). Arlington, VA: American Psychiatric Association.

The Diva. (July 1, 2004). *Essence* Revisits the Down Low. Blogcritics. http://www.blogcritics.org/essence-revisits-the-down-low

Elkins, R. & King, D. (1996). *Blending Genders: Social Aspects of Cross-Dressing and Sex-Changing*. London: Routledge.

Harris, E. L., Roberts, T., & Bandele, A. (July, 2004). Passing for Straight. *Essence, 35*(3), 156-210.

Henslin, J. M. (1998). *Essentials of Sociology: A Down-to-Earth Approach.* Boston: Pearson.

Humphreys, L. (1970). *Tearoom Trade: Impersonal Sex in Public Places.* New Brunswick, NJ: Aldine.

Jones, J. H. (1997). *Alfred C. Kinsey: A Life*. New York: W. W. Norton.

King, J. L. (2004). *On the Down Low: A Journey into the Lives of "Straight" Black Men Who Sleep with Men.* New York: Broadway Books.

Kinsey, A. C., Pomeroy, W. B., & Martin, C. E. (2010). *Sexual Behavior in the Human Male: Volume One*. Bronx, NY: Ishi Press International.

Lindsey, L. L. & Beach, S. (2000). *Sociology: Social Life and Social Issues.* Upper Saddle River, NJ: Prentice Hall.

Reinisch, J. M., Beasley, R., Kent, D., & Kinsey Institute. (1990). *The Kinsey Institute New Report on Sex: What You Must Do to Be Sexually Literate.* New York: St. Martin's Press.

Resnick, R., Halliday, D. & Krane, K. S. (1992). *Physics. Volume 1.* (4th ed.). New York: John Wiley & Sons.

Snowden, R. (2006). *Teach Yourself Freud.* Chicago: Contemporary Books.

Thomas, W. I., & Thomas, D. S. (1928). *The Child in America: Behavior Problems and Programs.* New York: Knopf.

Notes

An African American Images Publication

$15.95 USA * $17.95 CAN

Relationshi

Don't Hate the Player Learn the Game
How to Spot Ineligible Eligible Bachelors

Frequently Asked Questions:

*Why do some men avoid commitment?
*How can women distinguish the real from the counterfeit?
*What are the 9 types of players?
*Are you raising your son to be a player?
*Are you raising your daughter to be played?
*Can a player change?
*Do you want to choose the right mate?
*Do you believe you deserve better?

Lyn Lewis, PhD was Chair of the Sociology Department at the Universit of Detroit Mercy for more than 20 years. In addition to earning a PhD i sociology, this sociologist is also a licensed therapist, motivational speaker evaluator, trainer, researcher, and consultant. Dr. Lewis has been the re cipient of numerous awards, including the Faculty Award for Excellenc in the College of Liberal Arts at the University of Detroit. Dr. Lewis is a Adjunct Professor at Wayne County Community College District.

Contact Information:
http://www.AfricanAmericanImages.com
or
Customersvc@AfricanAmericanImages.com